Power Maths

Year 3
Practice Book 3B

White Rose Maths

White Rose Maths Edition

Imagine you had £100. What would you buy?

Draw it.

T0385787

This book belongs to _____ .

My class is _____ .

Series editor: Tony Staneff Lead author: Josh Lury

Consultants (first edition): Professor Liu Jian and Professor Zhang Dan

Author team (first edition): Tony Staneff, Josh Lury, David Board, Belle Cottingham, Jonathan East, Tim Handley, Derek Huby, Neil Jarrett and Timothy Weal

Contents

This looks like a good challenge!

It is time to do some practice!

How to use this book

Do you remember how to use this **Practice Book**?

Use the **Textbook** first to learn how to solve this type of problem.

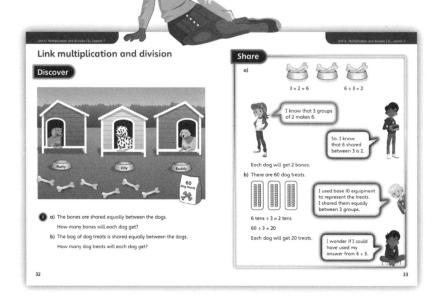

This shows you which **Textbook** page to use.

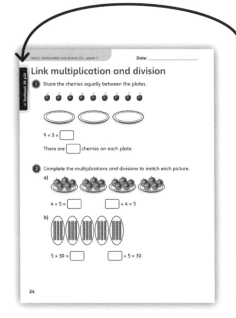

Have a go at questions by yourself using this **Practice Book**. Use what you have learnt.

Challenge questions make you think hard!

Questions with this light bulb make you think differently.

Reflect

Each lesson ends with a **Reflect** question so you can think about what you have learnt.

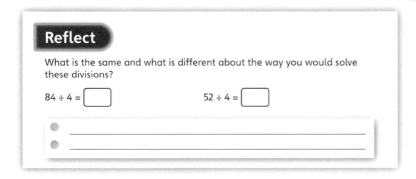

Use **My power points** at the back of this book to keep track of what you have learnt.

My journal

At the end of a unit your teacher will ask you to fill in **My journal**.

This will help you show how much you can do now that you have finished the unit.

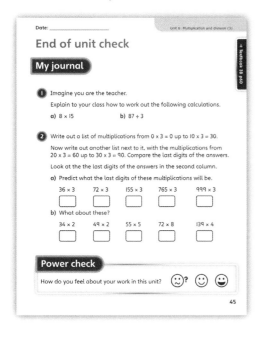

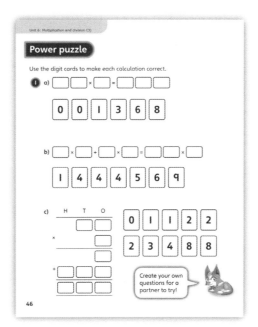

Date: _____

Multiples of 10

1 Write each multiple of 10.

a)
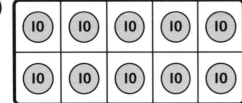

b)
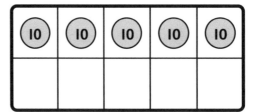

c)
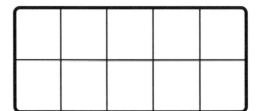

2 Draw more counters in the ten frames to show 240.

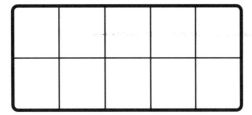

3 Match each multiplication to the correct place value grid.

| 54 × 10 | 45 × 10 | 51 × 10 | 10 × 41 |

H	T	O
5	1	0

H	T	O
5	4	0

H	T	O
4	1	0

H	T	O
4	5	0

4 Shade the multiples of 10 to find a path from the start to the finish.

15	190	250	130	105	90	480	30
50	500	5	110	70	40	202	180
150	99	408	17	175	104	97	400
280	360	41	440	180	140	10	340
302	520	197	80	56	65	901	604
140	600	81	160	572	20	100	60
230	65	532	200	310	150	256	220
90	99	101	307	66	428	999	80

Start ... Finish

5 Work out each multiple of 10.

CHALLENGE

a)

b)

c)

Reflect

Complete the sentence below.

I can tell if a number is a multiple of 10 by _____

_____

_____

8

Related calculations

1 How many pins are there?

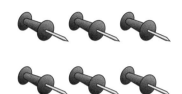

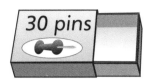

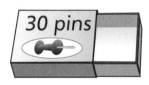

a) $2 \times 3 = \boxed{}$

There are $\boxed{}$ pins.

b) $2 \times 30 = \boxed{}$

There are $\boxed{}$ pins.

2 What is the score for each player?

Player 1

Player 2

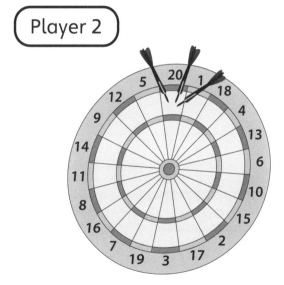

a) $\boxed{} \times \boxed{} = \boxed{}$

Player 1's score is $\boxed{}$.

b) $\boxed{} \times \boxed{} = \boxed{}$

Player 2's score is $\boxed{}$.

3 What multiplication calculations can you see?

a)

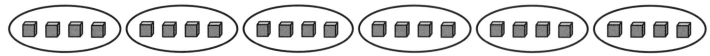

☐ × ☐ = ☐

b)

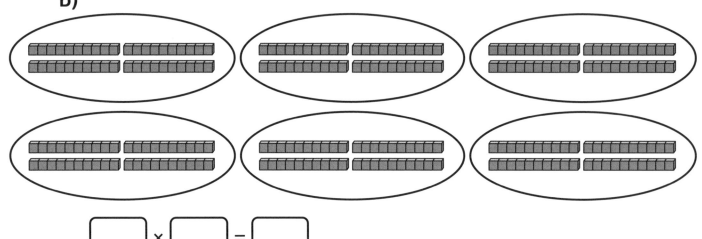

☐ × ☐ = ☐

4 Jamie and Richard each have some money.

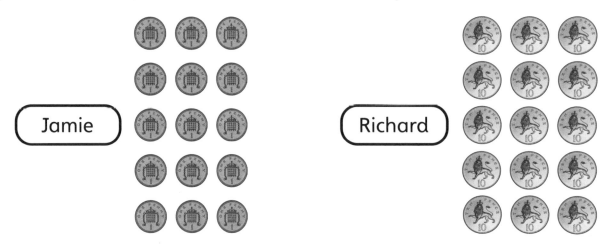

a) How much does Jamie have?

☐ × ☐ = ☐

b) How much does Richard have?

☐ × ☐ = ☐

5 Fill in numbers to make the multiplications correct.

a) 6 × 4 = ⬚

6 × 40 = ⬚

b) 9 × 5 = ⬚

9 × 50 = ⬚

c) 12 × 30 = ⬚

8 × 30 = ⬚

9 × 30 = ⬚

30 × 5 = ⬚

d) ⬚ = 4 × 20

⬚ = 20 × 8

⬚ = 0 × 20

⬚ = 11 × 20

6 Work out the answer to Holly's problem.

CHALLENGE

If I multiply my number by 5, I get 35. What do I get if I multiply my number by 50?

Explain how you got your answer.

_____

_____

Reflect

- I have learnt that if I know 4 × 8, I can work out 4 × 80 by _____
- _____
- _____

Date: _____

Reasoning about multiplication

1 Who has fewer biscuits?

Aki

Bella

5 × 10 ◯ 6 × 10

2 Compare the following statements using <, > or =.

Try to complete them without working out the multiplications.

a) 8 × 5 ◯ 10 × 5

b) 3 × 3 ◯ 3 × 1

c) 4 × 10 ◯ 8 × 5

d) 7 × 2 ◯ 9 × 2

3 Fill in numbers to make the sentences correct.

Try to estimate the answers before completing the calculations.

a) 5 × 3 > ◻ × 3

b) 9 × 4 = ◻ × 9

c) 12 × ◻ > 12 × 4

4 Are there more mints in total in the tubes or in the bags?

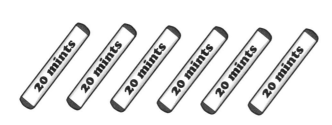

$$6 \times 20 \bigcirc 7 \times 20$$

There are more mints in total in the _____ .

5 Write <, > or = to make the statement correct.

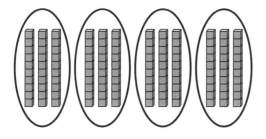
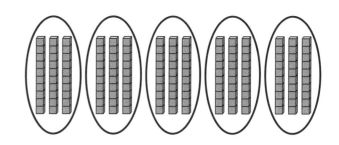

$$4 \times 30 \bigcirc 5 \times 30$$

6 Write <, > or = to make the statement correct.

a) $3 \times 50 \bigcirc 7 \times 50$

b) $4 \times 80 \bigcirc 4 \times 20$

c) $50 \times 4 \bigcirc 3 \times 50$

7

$5 \times 3 = 15$

$3 \times 3 = 9$

$2 \times 3 = 6$

I think there are different ways you can use the facts.

CHALLENGE

Use the above facts to work out

$8 \times 3 = \boxed{}$

$7 \times 3 = \boxed{}$

$9 \times 3 = \boxed{}$

Explain to a partner how you worked them out.

Reflect

Discuss this puzzle with a partner. Can you find more than one answer?

$$\bigcirc \times 5 > \boxed{} \times 8$$

Date: _____

Multiply 2-digits by 1-digit – no exchange

1 How many pencils in total?

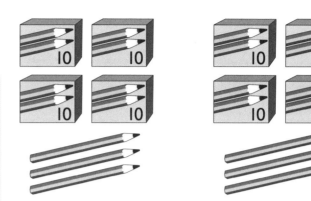

T	O

2 Work out 22 × 4.

15

3 Use the place value grids to work out the following multiplications.

a) 32 × 3

T	O
(10) (10) (10)	(1) (1)
(10) (10) (10)	(1) (1)
(10) (10) (10)	(1) (1)

So, 32 × 3 = ☐

b) 34 × 2

T	O
(10) (10) (10)	(1) (1) (1) (1)
(10) (10) (10)	(1) (1) (1) (1)

So, 34 × 2 = ☐

4 Find the solution to these calculations.

a) 14 × 2 = ☐   **b)** 3 × 33 = ☐

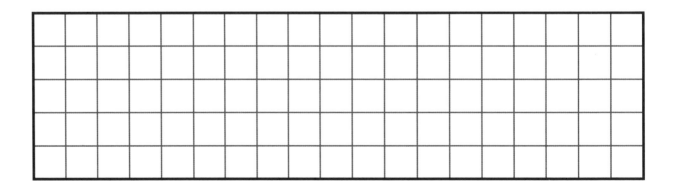

5 Olivia uses a different method to work out answers.

a) Use Olivia's method to work out 2 × 23.

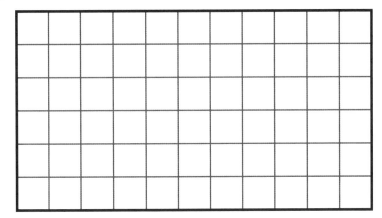

> I multiply the 10s and then the 1s and then add them together.

b) Work these out mentally.

24 × 2 = ☐

32 × 3 = ☐

2 × 43 = ☐

> My method helps me work out the answers in my head.

Reflect

In order to work out 3 × 13, first I would _____

_____

Then I would _____

_____

Finally I would _____

_____

Date: _____

Multiply 2-digits by 1-digit – exchange

1 Work out the answer to each of these multiplications.

a) 3 × 24 = ⬚

T	O
▦▦	⬚⬚⬚⬚
▦▦	⬚⬚⬚⬚
▦▦	⬚⬚⬚⬚

c) 2 × 28 = ⬚

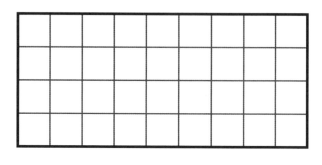

b) 5 × 13 = ⬚

T	O
▦	⬚⬚⬚
▦	⬚⬚⬚
▦	⬚⬚⬚
▦	⬚⬚⬚
▦	⬚⬚⬚

d) 4 × 36 = ⬚

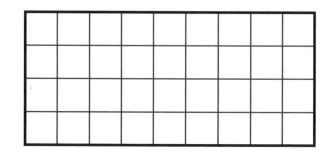

2 Use the place value grids to work out the following multiplications.

a) 35 × 3

b) 4 × 25

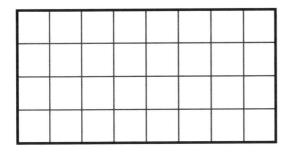

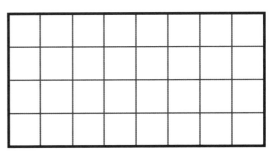

3 Work out the following calculations.

a) 3 × 26 = ☐

b) 6 × 14 = ☐

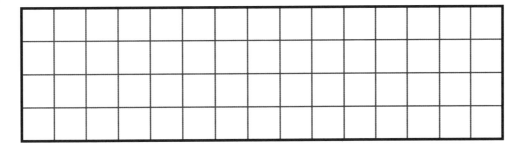

4 How much paint is there in total in 33 tins?

5 litres

5 Complete the multiplications using the working out calculations.

a)
> 3 × 7 = 21
> 3 × 10 = 30

$3 \times \boxed{} = 51$

b)
> 18 + 80 = 98

$2 \times \boxed{} = 98$

6 Match each multiplication to its answer.

Can you match them without working out the answers?

CHALLENGE

| 56 × 3 |
| 26 × 8 |
| 37 × 5 |

| 208 |
| 185 |
| 168 |

Reflect

What is the same and what is different about these calculations?

$36 \times 4 = \boxed{}$

$72 \times 2 = \boxed{}$

Expanded written method

1   Work out the answer to each of these multiplications.

a) 25 × 3

T	O
(base-ten rods)	*(ones)*
(base-ten rods)	*(ones)*
(base-ten rods)	*(ones)*

	T	O			
	2	5			
×		3			
			5	×	3
+			20	×	3

b) 17 × 4

T	O
10	1 1 1 1 1 / 1 1
10	1 1 1 1 1 / 1 1
10	1 1 1 1 1 / 1 1
10	1 1 1 1 1 / 1 1

	T	O			
	1	7			
×		4			
			7	×	4
+			10	×	4

2   Work out the following multiplications.

a) 16 × 3

	T	O
	1	6
×		3
+		

b) 48 × 2

	T	O
	4	8
×		2
+		

3 Work out the multiplications using a column method.

a) $14 \times 5 = \boxed{}$

b) $4 \times 19 = \boxed{}$

4 Ambika used these digits to make a multiplication.

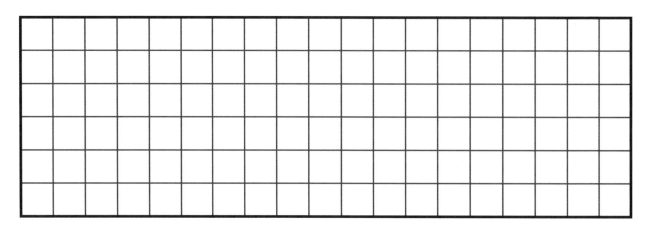

| 1 | 2 | 4 |

Work out where the digits go in each multiplication.

a)

	T	O
×		
		8
+	4	0

b)

	T	O
×		
		4
+	8	0

5 Jamie is working out 26×1.

Could Jamie have worked it out an easier way?
Explain how.

_____

_____

_____

		T	O
		2	6
×			1
			6
+		2	0
		2	6

6 Work out the following multiplications.

a) 35 × 3

	H	T	O
		3	5
×			3
+			

b) 18 × 6

	H	T	O
		1	8
×			6
+			

7 Work out the answer to the following multiplication.

CHALLENGE

I will try to work out what each symbol is worth first.

Explain your reasoning.

_____

_____

_____

	H	T	O
		⬤	⬤
×			3
		△	⬤
+	△	⬤	♥

Reflect

Explain how to set out and complete 23 × 5 using the column method.

- _____
- _____
- _____

23

Date: _____

Link multiplication and division

1 Share the cherries equally between the plates.

$9 \div 3 = \boxed{}$

There are $\boxed{}$ cherries on each plate.

2 Complete the multiplications and divisions to match each picture.

a)

$4 \times 5 = \boxed{}$ $\boxed{} \div 4 = 5$

b)

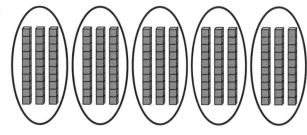

$5 \times 30 = \boxed{}$ $\boxed{} \div 5 = 30$

3 Complete each fact family.

a)

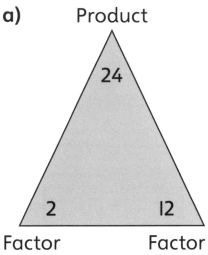

Product

24

2   12

Factor   Factor

12 × 2 = ☐

2 × 12 = ☐

☐ ÷ ☐ = 12

☐ ÷ ☐ = 2

b)

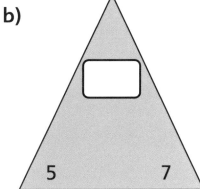

☐ × ☐ = ☐

☐ × ☐ = ☐

☐ ÷ ☐ = ☐

☐ ÷ ☐ = ☐

c)

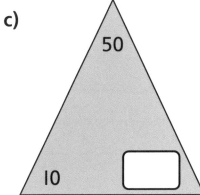

☐ × ☐ = ☐

☐ × ☐ = ☐

☐ ÷ ☐ = ☐

☐ ÷ ☐ = ☐

4 What multiplication and division facts can you see?

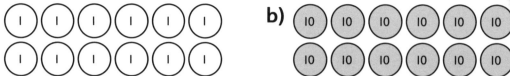

a)

$\boxed{} \times \boxed{} = \boxed{}$

$\boxed{} \times \boxed{} = \boxed{}$

$\boxed{} \div \boxed{} = \boxed{}$

$\boxed{} \div \boxed{} = \boxed{}$

b)

$\boxed{} \times \boxed{} = \boxed{}$

$\boxed{} \times \boxed{} = \boxed{}$

$\boxed{} \div \boxed{} = \boxed{}$

$\boxed{} \div \boxed{} = \boxed{}$

Reflect

I know $8 \times 3 = 24$, so I also know that _____

_____

_____

_____

_____

Divide 2-digits by 1-digit – no exchange

1 Share 28 apples equally between 2 baskets.

There are ☐ apples in each basket.

2 Work out 69 ÷ 3.

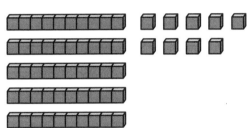

69 ÷ 3 = ☐

3 Work out 88 ÷ 4.

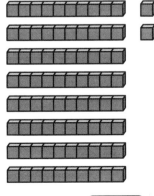
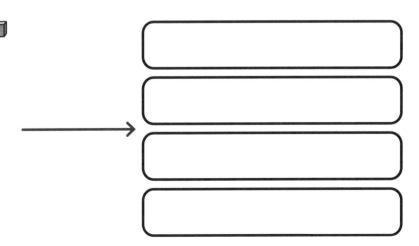

88 ÷ 4 = ☐

Complete each division.

a) $26 \div 2 = \boxed{}$

b) $36 \div 3 = \boxed{}$

c) $40 \div 2 = \boxed{}$

d) $64 \div 2 = \boxed{}$

5 There are 39 apples in a box. They are divided equally into 3 bags.

How many apples are in each bag?

6 Work out the missing numbers in these divisions.

CHALLENGE

a) [ ] ÷ 2 = 32

b) [ ] ÷ 3 = 32

c) [ ] ÷ 2 = 22

d) [ ] ÷ 3 = 22

Reflect

Explain how you used your multiplication skills to help you divide.

_____

_____

_____

Date: _____

Divide 2-digits by 1-digit – flexible partitioning

 Work out the following divisions.

a) $45 \div 3 = \boxed{}$

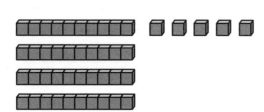 →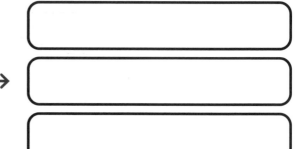

b) $34 \div 2 = \boxed{}$

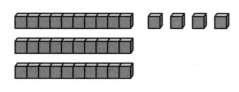 →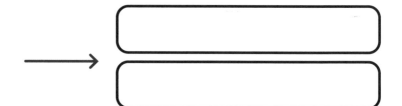

c) $52 \div 4 = \boxed{}$

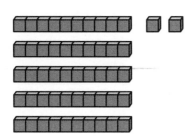 →

30

2 Work out the following divisions.

a) $72 \div 2 = \boxed{}$

b) $95 \div 5 = \boxed{}$

c) $72 \div 3 = \boxed{}$

d) $57 \div 3 = \boxed{}$

3 Mr Lopez has a tray of 84 cubes.

Each child needs 3 cubes.

There are 27 children in the class.

Are there enough cubes for each child to have 3?

4 Complete the missing numbers in these divisions.

a) ⬜ ÷ 3 = 26

b) ⬜ ÷ 5 = 17

c) ⬜ ÷ 4 = 19

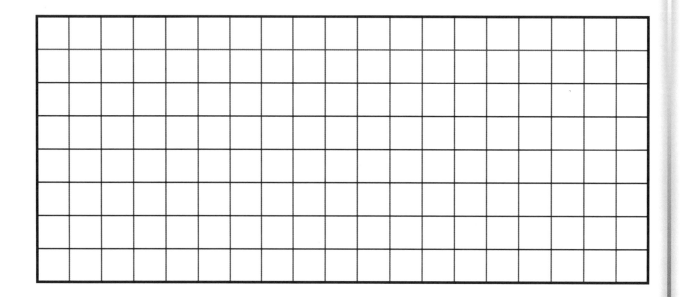

Reflect

What is the same and what is different about the way you would solve these divisions?

84 ÷ 4 = ⬜   52 ÷ 4 = ⬜

Divide 2-digits by 1-digit with remainders

 a) Divide 9 into 2 equal groups.

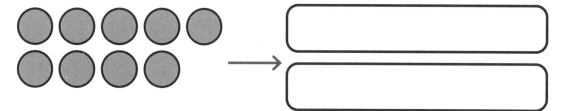

$9 \div 2 =$ ⬚ remainder ⬚

b) Divide 9 into 4 equal groups.

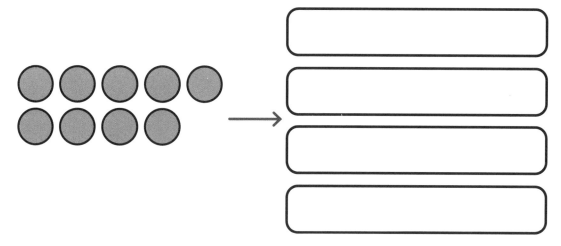

$9 \div 4 =$ ⬚ remainder ⬚

2 Calculate $10 \div 4$.

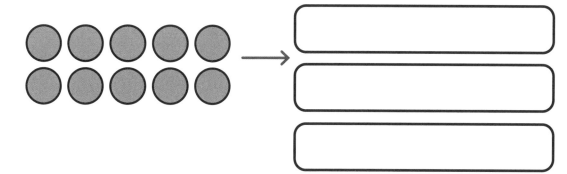

$10 \div 4 =$ ⬚ remainder ⬚

33

3 Complete each division.

a) $16 \div 3 =$ ☐ remainder ☐

b) $17 \div 3 =$ ☐ remainder ☐

c) $18 \div 3 =$ ☐ remainder ☐

4 Complete each division.

If there is a remainder, write it next to the answer box.

a) $25 \div 3 =$ ☐

b) $25 \div 4 =$ ☐

c) $25 \div 5 =$ ☐

d) $25 \div 6 =$ ☐

e) $25 \div 7 =$ ☐

f) $25 \div 8 =$ ☐

5 Will $57 \div 5$ have a remainder? Predict and then check.

I predict that _____

_____

_____

6

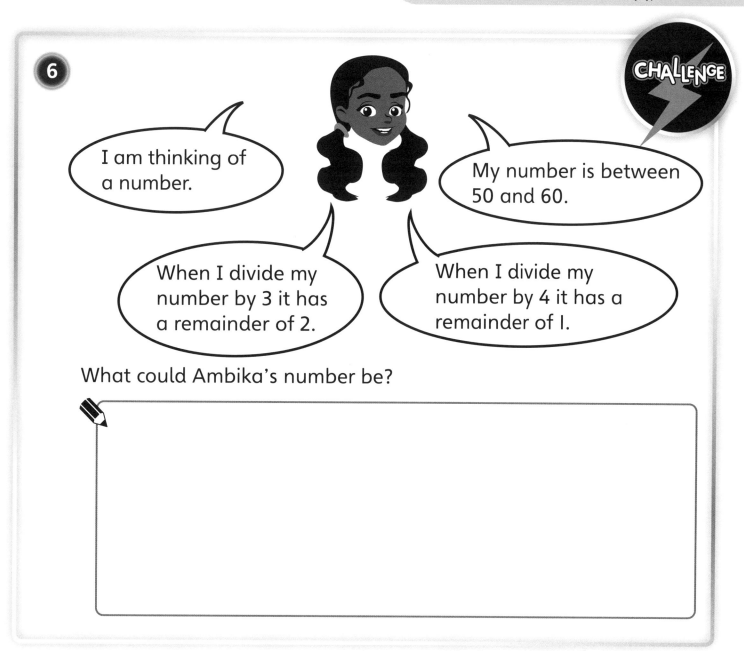

CHALLENGE

I am thinking of a number.

My number is between 50 and 60.

When I divide my number by 3 it has a remainder of 2.

When I divide my number by 4 it has a remainder of 1.

What could Ambika's number be?

Reflect

Which of these will have a remainder? How do you know?

24 ÷ 2   26 ÷ 2   27 ÷ 2   35 ÷ 2

Date: _____

How many ways?

1 Bella needs some glasses and shoes.

There are 3 pairs of glasses and 3 pairs of shoes she can choose from.

A   B  C

1  2  3

a) List all the possible ways Bella can choose the glasses and shoes. (You may not need to use all of the rows below.)

Glasses	Shoes

Glasses	Shoes

b) What multiplication will help you calculate the total number of different ways?

⬜ × ⬜ = ⬜

There are ⬜ ways.

Do you see a link between the number of items and the number of ways?

2 Richard has 5 symbol cards and 2 letter cards.

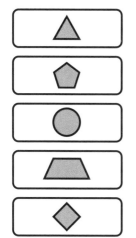

Richard picks a symbol card and a letter card.

a) How many different ways could he do this?

$\boxed{} \times \boxed{} = \boxed{}$

There are $\boxed{}$ ways.

b) Show all the ways in the tables below.

Symbol	Letter

Symbol	Letter

Symbol	Letter

c) Richard now has 6 symbol cards and 4 letter cards.

He picks a symbol card and a letter card.

How many different possible ways could he do this?

There are $\boxed{}$ ways.

3 Zac picks a piece of fruit and a snack.

How many different ways could he do this?

There are ☐ ways.

Fruit   Snacks

4 Choose 3 different colouring pencils.

CHALLENGE

A flag is made up of 2 different colours and is divided in half vertically.

How many different flags can you make, using all 3 of your colouring pencils?

I can make ☐ flags.

Explain your answer.

_____

_____

Reflect

To work out the number of ways in question 3, I would _____

_____

Problem solving – mixed problems

1 There are 15 cakes on a tray.

How many cakes are there on 3 trays?

```
            ?
┌─────────┬─────────┬─────────┐
│   15    │   15    │   15    │
└─────────┴─────────┴─────────┘
```

There are ☐ cakes in total.

2 There are 64 items of clothing in this chest of drawers.

There is the same number of items in each drawer.

How many items of clothing are in each drawer?

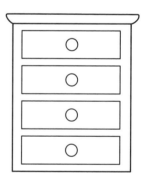

```
            64
┌─────┬─────┬─────┬─────┐
│     │     │     │     │
└─────┴─────┴─────┴─────┘
```

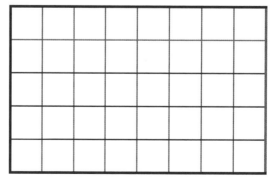

There are ☐ items of clothing in each drawer.

3 **a)** A jar contains 8 spoonfuls of honey.

Each spoonful holds 12 ml of honey.

How much honey is in the jar?

There are ☐ ml of honey in the jar.

b) The honey is poured equally onto 3 bowls of porridge.

How much honey is in each bowl?

There are ☐ ml of honey in each bowl.

4 A tower is 3 times as tall as a house.

A house is 34 metres tall.

How tall is the tower?

The tower is ☐ metres tall.

5 Work out the missing number.

$26 \times 3 = \boxed{} \times 2$

Use the bar model to help you.

26	26	26

6 5 books cost £85.

£85

Each book costs the same. How much do 2 of the books cost?

2 books cost £ $\boxed{}$.

Reflect

Max used this bar model to help him solve a problem.

What could the problem have been?

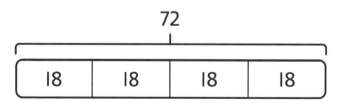

72

18	18	18	18

41

Date: _____

Problem solving – mixed problems ❷

1 Ice creams are sold in boxes of 3 or boxes of 5.

Ebo buys the following ice creams.

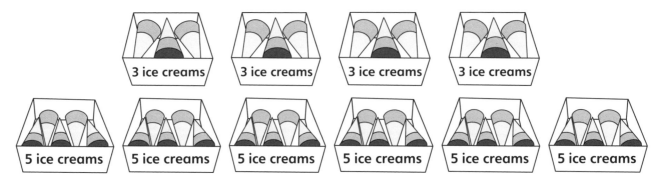

3 ice creams   3 ice creams   3 ice creams   3 ice creams

5 ice creams   5 ice creams   5 ice creams   5 ice creams   5 ice creams   5 ice creams

How many ice creams does he buy in total?

Ebo buys [   ] ice creams in total.

2 A basket contains 5 apples and 8 pears.

There are 7 baskets.

How many more pears than apples are there?

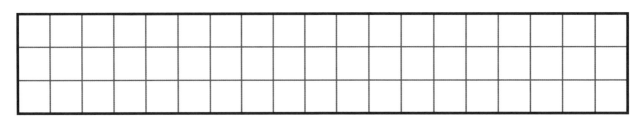

There are [   ] more pears than apples.

42

3 A bag of balloons contains 5 red and 3 blue balloons.

a) How many balloons in 6 bags?

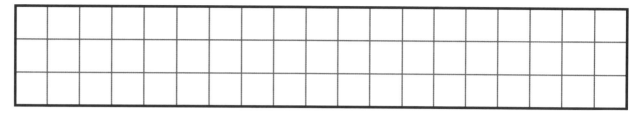

There are ☐ balloons in 6 bags.

b) Reena needs 80 balloons for a birthday party.

How many bags does she need to buy?

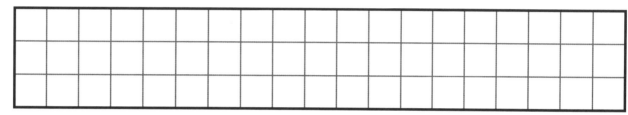

Reena needs to buy ☐ bags.

4 Rulers are sold in boxes of 5.

Mrs Dean has 3 boxes of rulers.
Mr Jones has 4 boxes of rulers.

Work out how many rulers they have altogether.

5	5	5

Mrs Dean

5	5	5	5

Mr Jones

$3 \times 5 + 4 \times 5 = $ ☐ $\times 5$

They have ☐ rulers altogether.

43

5 Work out the missing numbers.

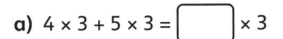

Use a bar model to help you.

a) $4 \times 3 + 5 \times 3 = \boxed{} \times 3$

b) $8 \times 5 + \boxed{} \times 5 = 12 \times 5$

c) $3 \times 8 + 8 = \boxed{} \times 8$

d) $7 \times 4 - 2 \times 4 = \boxed{} \times 4$

e) $5 \times 2 + 8 = \boxed{} \times 2$

CHALLENGE

6 2 eggs and a slice of toast cost 60 pence.

2 eggs and 3 slices of toast cost 96 pence.

Work out the cost of an egg.

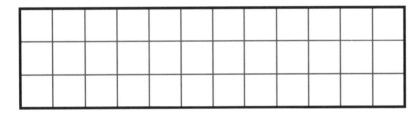

The cost of an egg is $\boxed{}$ pence.

Reflect

A box contains 5 yellow counters and 3 blue counters.

There are 6 boxes of these counters.

Explain two ways you can work out the total number of counters.

- _____
- _____
- _____

End of unit check

My journal

1. Imagine you are the teacher.

Explain to a partner how to work out the following calculations.

a) 8 × 15

b) 87 ÷ 3

2. Write out a list of multiplications from 0 x 3 = 0 up to 10 x 3 = 30.

Now write out another list next to it, with the multiplications from 20 x 3 = 60 up to 30 x 3 = 90. Compare the last digits of the answers.

a) Predict what the last digits of these multiplications will be.

36 × 3	72 × 3	155 × 3	765 × 3	999 × 3
☐	☐	☐	☐	☐

b) What about these?

34 × 2	49 × 2	55 × 5	72 × 8	139 × 4
☐	☐	☐	☐	☐

Power check

How do you feel about your work in this unit?

Power puzzle

Use the digit cards to make each calculation correct.

1 **a)** ▢▢ × ▢ = ▢▢▢

0	0	1	3	6	8

b) ▢ × ▢ + ▢ × ▢ = ▢▢ × ▢

1	4	4	4	5	6	9

c)

	H	T	O

0	1	1	2	2

2	3	4	8	8

Create your own questions for a partner to try!

Date: _____

Measure in m and cm

1 **a)** How long is the shark?

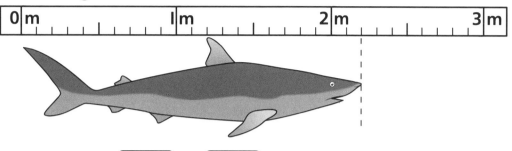

The shark is ☐ m ☐ cm long.

b) How long is the dolphin?

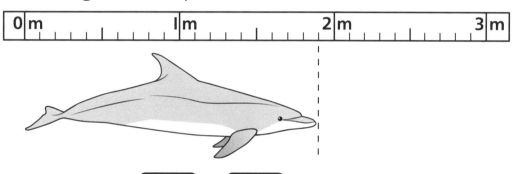

The dolphin is ☐ m ☐ cm long.

c) How long is the swordfish?

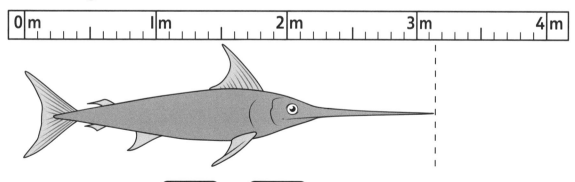

The swordfish is ☐ m ☐ cm long.

d) A fish is 95 cm long. Mark its length on the ruler below.

→ Textbook 3B p64

2 Measure the arm span of three people in your class.

Name	Arm span

Arm span

3 Mark has measured this line as 60 cm. Explain his mistake.

_____

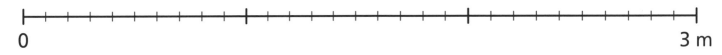

_____

_____

_____

4 Draw arrows to mark these measurements.

a)
50 cm

b)
1 m 10 cm

c)
1 m 90 cm

d)
2 m 75 cm

0   3 m

5 Find things in your classroom that are these lengths.
Complete the table.

	Item	Length
Under 1 m		
Between 1 m and 1 m 50 cm		
Between 2 m and 3 m		

6 Ebo thinks the line he has drawn on the playground is 1 m 10 cm long.
How could he check?

CHALLENGE

_____
_____
_____

Reflect

How could you accurately measure your height?

_____
_____
_____

Date: _____

Measure in cm and mm

1 What measurements are shown?

a)

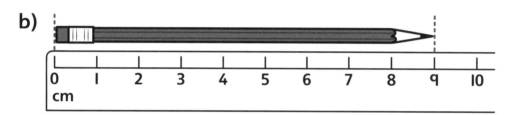

The toy car is [   ] mm long.

b)

The pencil is [   ] cm long.

c)

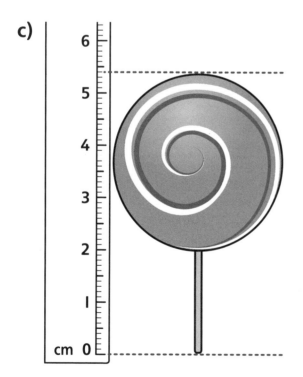

The lollipop is [   ] cm and [   ] mm tall.

50

2 Use a ruler to draw lines that measure

   a) 3 cm   **b)** 56 mm   **c)** 4 cm and 8 mm

3 Measure these lines.

Give your answers in mm.

a) ⬭ mm

b) ⬭ mm

c) ⬭ mm

4 Measure the length of these objects using a ruler.

Write the measurements in cm and mm.

Object				
Pencil	☐	cm	☐	mm
Book	☐	cm	☐	mm
Glue stick	☐	cm	☐	mm
Rubber	☐	cm	☐	mm

5 **a)** Andy wants to measure the lengths of an elephant and a mouse. Explain which units of measure he should use for each animal and why.

CHALLENGE

I think Andy could use metres, centimetres or millimetres!

_____

_____

_____

_____

b) List some other items you could measure in centimetres or millimetres.

Centimetres	Millimetres

Reflect

Explain how to measure accurately using cm and mm.

- To measure accurately you must _____

  _____

Metres, centimetres and millimetres

1 Match each item to its correct measurement.

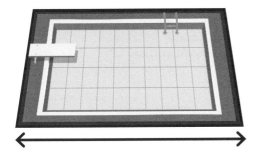

 10 m

10 cm

10 mm

2 Write mm, cm or m to complete the measurements.

a)

The length of the book

is 23 [   ].

b)

The height of the football

goal is 2 [   ].

c)

The height of the cup

is 8 [   ].

d)

The width of the pencil

sharpener is 23 [   ].

3 Complete the bar models.

a)

1 m
☐ cm

1 m is ☐ cm

b)

4 m			
☐ cm	☐ cm	☐ cm	☐ cm

4 m is ☐ cm

4 a)

1 cm
☐ mm

1 cm is ☐ mm

b)

3 cm		
☐ mm	☐ mm	☐ mm

3 cm is ☐ mm

c)

4 cm			
☐ mm	☐ mm	☐ mm	☐ mm

4 cm is ☐ mm

5 **a)** A piece of string is 80 mm long.

How many cm is this? ▢ cm

b) A tree is 700 cm tall.

How many metres is this? ▢ m

CHALLENGE

6 Write the missing measurements.

500 cm is ▢ m

900 cm is ▢ m

9 cm is ▢ mm

5 cm is ▢ mm

▢ cm is 7 m

▢ cm is 8 m

▢ cm is 70 mm

▢ cm is 100 mm

Reflect

Something that might be 7 mm long is a _____.

Something that might be 7 cm long is a _____.

Something that might be 7 m long is a _____.

Date: _____

Equivalent lengths (m and cm)

1 **a)** Aki jumped 145 cm.

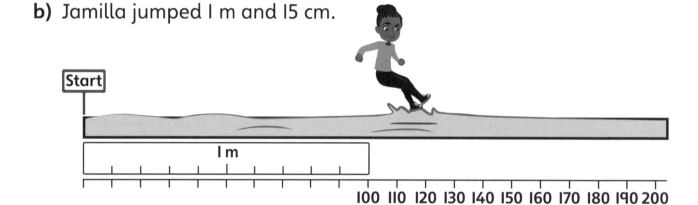

Start

| 1 m |
| cm |

100 110 120 130 140 150

Aki jumped ☐ m and ☐ cm.

b) Jamilla jumped 1 m and 15 cm.

Start

| 1 m |

100 110 120 130 140 150 160 170 180 190 200
cm

Jamilla jumped ☐ cm.

c) Jamie jumped 167 cm.

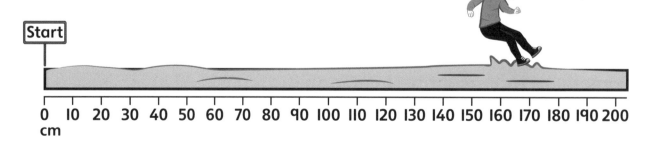

Start

0 10 20 30 40 50 60 70 80 90 100 110 120 130 140 150 160 170 180 190 200
cm

Jamie jumped ☐ m ☐ cm.

2 Complete the bar models.

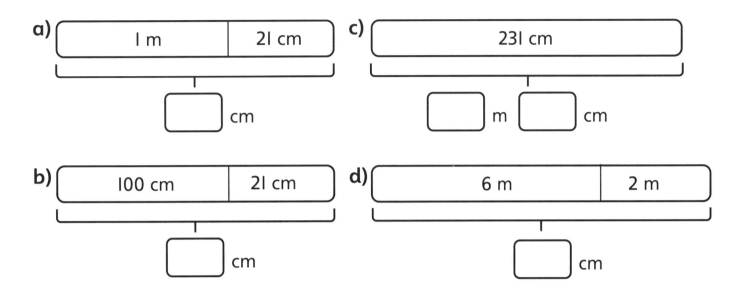

a)

1 m	21 cm

☐ cm

c)

231 cm

☐ m ☐ cm

b)

100 cm	21 cm

☐ cm

d)

6 m	2 m

☐ cm

3 Complete the table.

5 m 30 cm	☐ cm
☐ m ☐ cm	673 cm
3 m 3 cm	☐ cm
0 m 23 cm	☐ cm

4 Filip says 2 m 4 cm is 240 cm. Explain why this is wrong.

_____

_____

_____

57

5 Play this game with a partner. Take turns.

Choose a box and say the length in centimetres.

If you say it correctly, draw a line through it.

The first player to get three boxes lined up (in a row, a column or diagonally) wins.

CHALLENGE

5 m 32 cm	0 m 10 cm	7 m 64 cm	0 m 0 cm
3 m 43 cm	5 m 74 cm	9 m 32 cm	0 m 75 cm
0 m 26 cm	3 m 12 cm	1 m 10 cm	8 m 46 cm
0 m 56 cm	4 m 7 cm	0 m 1 cm	3 m
6 m 32 cm	0 m 45 cm	3 m 65 cm	0 m 64 cm

Reflect

3 m

7 m 22 cm

243 cm

Pick a measurement and explain how to convert it to an equivalent length.

Date: _____

Equivalent lengths (mm and cm)

↓ Textbook 3B p80

1 Luis wants to cut some string.

He needs some help measuring.

a) Mark 2 cm 5 mm on the ruler.

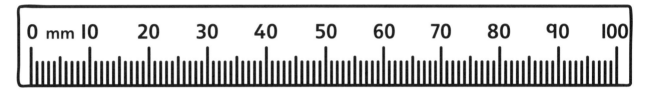

b) Mark 30 mm on the ruler.

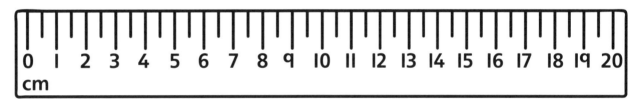

c) Mark 9 cm 9 mm on the ruler.

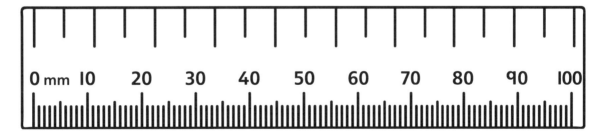

d) Mark 1 mm on the ruler.

2 Complete the bar models.

a)

38 mm	
☐ cm	☐ mm

b)

☐ mm	
l cm	l mm

c)

75 mm	
☐ cm	☐ mm

3 Complete this table.

I need to be careful about place value of each digit in these questions.

7 cm 22 mm	☐ mm
☐ cm ☐ mm	92 mm
3 cm 0 mm	☐ cm
2 cm 8l mm	☐ mm

60

4 Kate says there are no whole centimetres in 5 mm.

Is she correct? Explain.

_____

_____

_____

_____

CHALLENGE

5 Work with a partner. Try to cut strips of paper that are exactly these lengths:

a) 67 mm

b) 9 cm 2 mm

c) 6 cm 7 mm

d) 121 mm

e) 8 cm 9 mm

Which two lengths are equal? _____ and _____

Reflect

Luis measures a really long piece of string. He writes down 765 mm. He then converts this measurement to 76 cm 5 mm.

Is it better to use millimetres, or centimetres and millimetres, for longer lengths? Why?

I think _____ are better because

_____

_____

Date: _____

Compare lengths

1 **a)** Mark on the ruler below where the four paper aeroplanes landed.

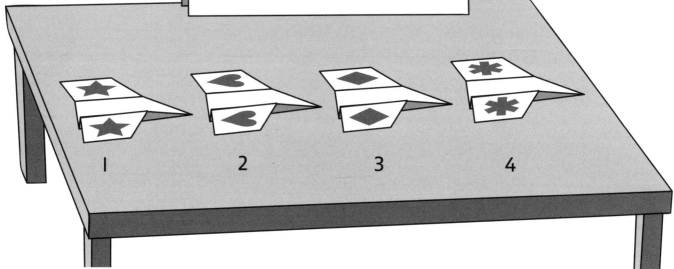

Distance flown

Plane 1: 5 m
Plane 2: 5 m 89 cm
Plane 3: 475 cm
Plane 4: 500 cm

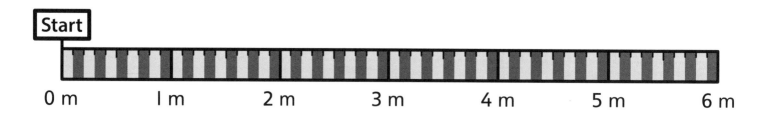

Start						
0 m	1 m	2 m	3 m	4 m	5 m	6 m

b) Which aeroplane flew the furthest? Plane ☐

c) Which aeroplane flew the shortest distance? Plane ☐

d) Which aeroplane flew between 4 and 5 metres? Plane ☐

2 Write <, > or = to complete the number sentences.

a) 12 cm $\bigcirc$ 48 cm

b) 13 cm $\bigcirc$ 13 m

c) 5 m 87 cm $\bigcirc$ 5 m 45 cm

d) 4 m 18 cm $\bigcirc$ 7 m 81 cm

e) 6 m $\bigcirc$ 5 m 98 cm

f) 7 m $\bigcirc$ 700 cm

g) 14 cm $\bigcirc$ 40 mm

h) 92 mm $\bigcirc$ 8 cm

3 Circle the longest length in each list.

a) 1 m 75 cm   and   167 cm

b) 3 m 4 cm   and   418 cm

c) 8 m 25 cm   and   890 cm

d) 118 cm,   2 m 19 cm   and   95 cm

e) 7 cm 2 mm   and   38 mm

f) 19 cm,   8 mm   and   240 mm

g) 9 cm 1 mm   and   45 cm 3 mm

4 Write the following lengths in order from shortest to longest.

200 cm   970 mm   1 m 95 cm   190 cm

Shortest _____   _____   _____   _____ Longest

63

5

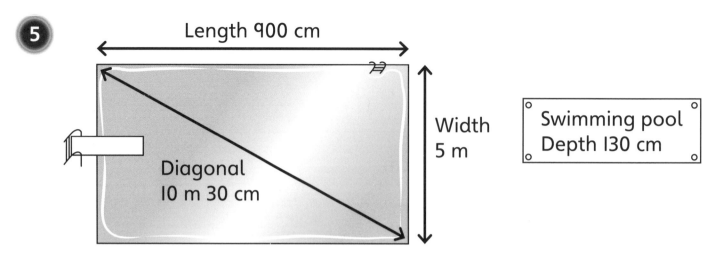

Length 900 cm

Diagonal
10 m 30 cm

Width
5 m

Swimming pool
Depth 130 cm

Complete these number sentences.

a) The longest distance you can swim in a straight line is

☐ m and ☐ cm.

b) The shortest distance from one corner of the pool to another is

☐ cm.

6 Which is longer, the pencil case or the box?

CHALLENGE

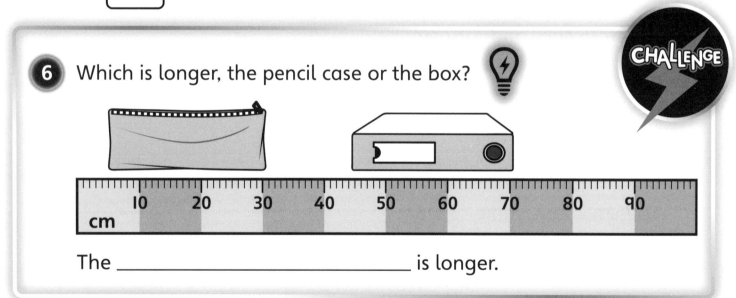

The _____ is longer.

Reflect

How would you order the lengths 3 m 8 cm, 380 cm and 380 mm?

Date: _____

Add lengths

1 What is the total length?

a)

 6 m

 3 m

6 m + 3 m = ☐ m

b)

 40 cm

 20 cm

40 cm + 20 cm = ☐ cm

2 What is the total length?

 120 cm

 65 cm

120 cm + 65 cm = ☐ cm

3 A shop displays a vase on a stand. What is the total height of the display?

The total height is _____.

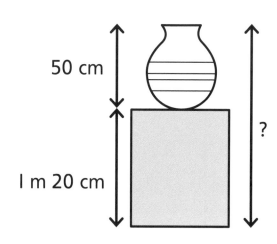

50 cm

1 m 20 cm

?

4 The shop has more displays of vases and stands. Complete the table.

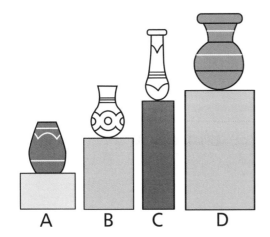

Display	Stand height	Vase height	Total height
A	40 cm	30 cm	
B	80 cm	30 cm	
C	1 m 20 cm	60 cm	
D	1 m 30 cm	70 cm	

5 Complete the number sentences.

a) 75 cm + 25 cm = ☐ m

c) 6 cm + 70 mm = ☐ cm

b) 27 mm + ☐ mm = 3 cm

d) 2 m 25 cm + ☐ cm = 3 m

6 Jamilla and Andy took part in a hop, skip and jump competition.

Jamilla hopped 80 cm, skipped 70 cm and jumped 1 m 20 cm.

Andy hopped 70 cm, skipped 1 m 10 cm and jumped 1 m.

Who won the competition?

7 These four books are stacked on top of each other. What is the total height of the stack of books?

CHALLENGE

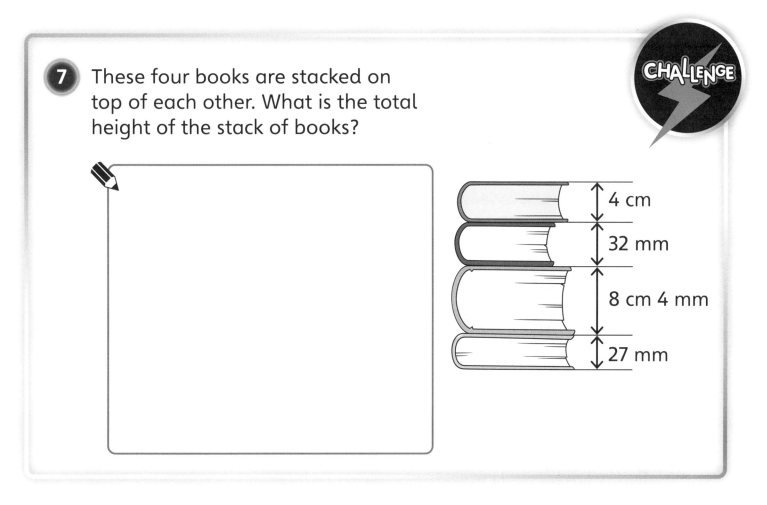

4 cm

32 mm

8 cm 4 mm

27 mm

Reflect

Mrs Dean asked Zac to work out the total length of two display boards.

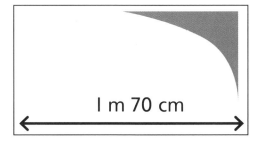

1 m 70 cm

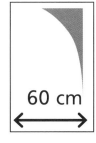

60 cm

When I add 60 cm to 1 m 70 cm, I get 1 m 130 cm.

Zac

Do you agree with Zac? Explain. _____

_____

Date: _____

Subtract lengths

↑ Textbook 3B p92

1 **a)** The pipe was 3 m 50 cm long. Jen has cut a 1 m piece off the end. How long is the pipe now?

3 m 50 cm

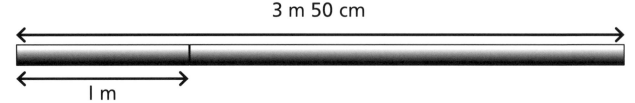

1 m

The pipe is now _____ long.

b) Toshi has a plank 3 m 50 cm long. He cuts off a piece 2 m long. How much of the plank is left?

3 m 50 cm

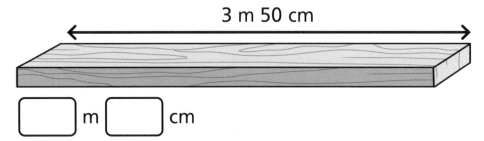

☐ m ☐ cm

c) A piece of string is 65 mm long. Aki cuts off 3 cm. How long is the string now?

65 mm

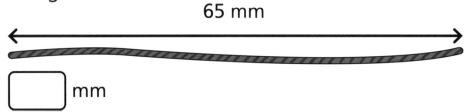

☐ mm

2 Work out

a) 362 cm – 145 cm   **b)** 185 m – 59 m

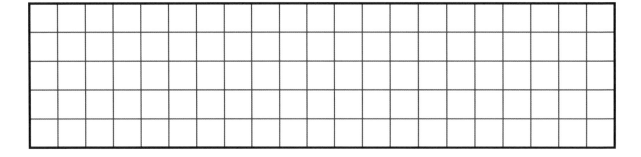

68

3 Sofia puts a flower in a vase.

The vase is I m 20 cm high and the flower is I m 40 cm high.

How far does the flower stick out above the vase?

The flower sticks out ▢ cm.

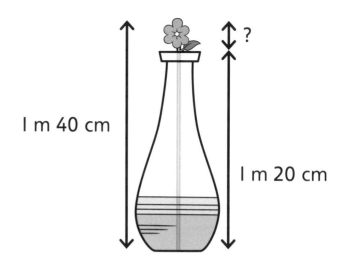

I m 40 cm

I m 20 cm

4 **a)** I m 10 cm – 50 cm = ▢

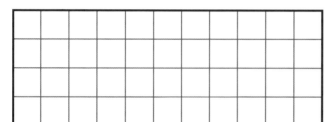

d) 85 mm – 2 cm = ▢

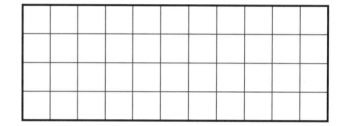

b) 318 cm – I m 70 cm = ▢

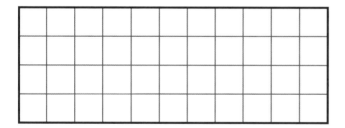

e) 5 cm 8 mm – 20 mm = ▢

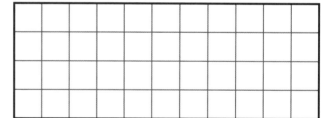

c) 350 cm – ▢ = 2 m 10 cm

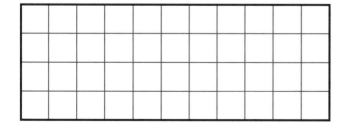

f) 2 cm 5 mm – 8 mm = ▢

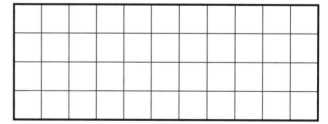

5 Reena bought a new 10 m reel of ribbon and used 2 m 50 cm of it.

She then lent the reel to Aki.

When Aki gave the reel back, there was 3 m 60 cm of ribbon left.

How much ribbon did Aki use?

CHALLENGE

Ribbon 10 m

Reena   Aki

Reflect

What method could you use to solve each of these subtractions?

3 m 30 cm – 165 cm   2 m – 1 m 30 cm

Measure perimeter

 a) Measure the sides of the rectangle.

Write on the measurements.

What is the perimeter
of the rectangle?

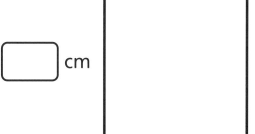

☐ cm

☐ cm

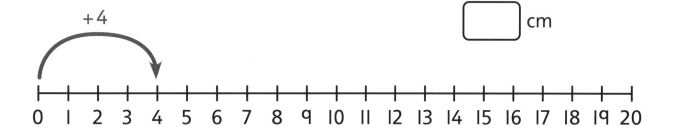

+4

The perimeter of the rectangle is ☐ cm.

b) Measure the perimeter of this triangle.

The perimeter of the triangle is ☐ cm.

c) Measure the perimeter of this square.

The square has a perimeter of ☐ cm.

2 Measure the perimeters of these shapes in mm.

a)

Perimeter = ☐ mm

b)
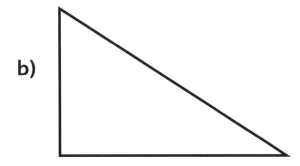

Perimeter = ☐ mm

c)
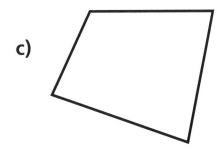

Perimeter = ☐ mm

3 Draw a shape with a perimeter of 8 cm.

1 cm

CHALLENGE

④ Order these shapes based on the lengths of their perimeters.

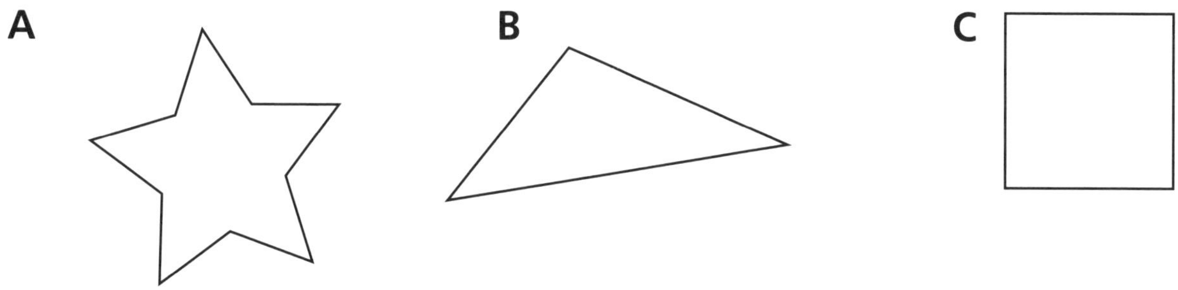

A

B

C

Shortest perimeter ――――――――→ Longest perimeter

Reflect

Explain how to find the perimeter of a shape.

Date: _____

Calculate perimeter

1 Work out the perimeter of each shape.

a)

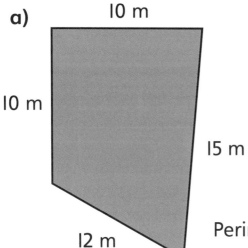

10 m

10 m

15 m

12 m

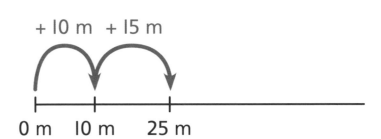

+ 10 m   + 15 m

0 m   10 m   25 m

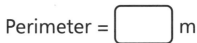

Perimeter = ☐ m

b)

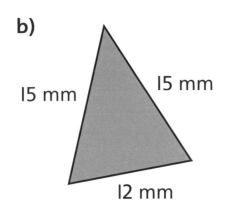

15 mm

15 mm

12 mm

Perimeter = ☐ mm

d)

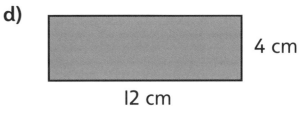

4 cm

12 cm

Perimeter = ☐ cm

c)

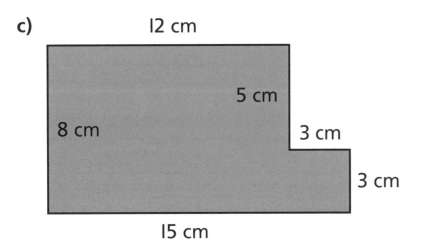

12 cm

5 cm

8 cm

3 cm

3 cm

15 cm

Perimeter = ☐ cm

74

2 Work out the missing lengths.

a) Perimeter: 37 cm   b) Perimeter: 30 m   c) Perimeter: 26 mm

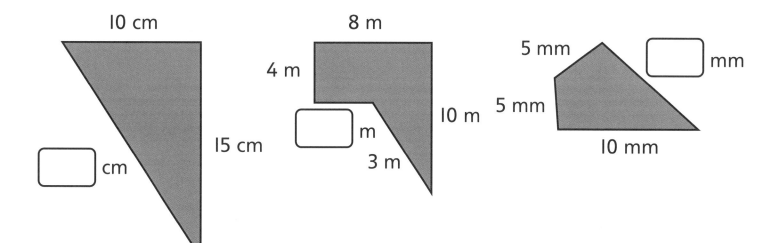

3 Here is a field.

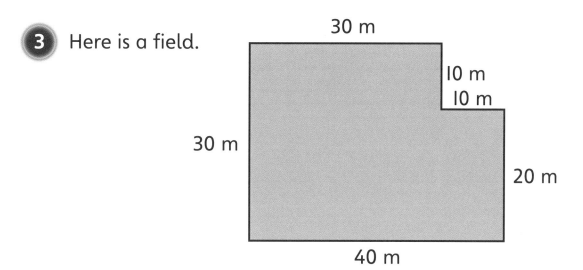

Work out the perimeter of the field.

4 Draw lines to match the items below with their most likely perimeter.

A piece of A4 paper

An interactive whiteboard

A football field

A £5 note

420 m

526 cm

380 mm

101 cm

> I wonder what units I should use to measure each item.

CHALLENGE

5 Work out the perimeter of the rectangle.

2 cm

4 cm

Perimeter = ☐ cm

Reflect

Explain how you can work out the perimeter of any shape if you know the lengths of its sides.

Problem solving – length

1 Luis swims 3 lengths of 25 metres each. How far does he swim?

25 m	25 m	25 m

?

25 × ☐ = ☐ Luis swims ☐ metres.

2 Emma cuts a 40 cm ribbon into 5 equal pieces.

How long is each piece?

40 cm

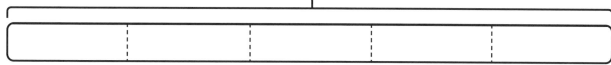

☐ ÷ ☐ = ☐

Each piece is ☐ cm.

3 A pastry has 9 cm of cream piped onto it. A baker can pipe 72 cm of cream in one minute. How many pastries is that?

☐ ÷ ☐ = ☐

The baker pipes ☐ pastries in one minute.

4 How much fence is needed to go all the way around this square school field?

20 m

Write the calculation you used.

_____

[ ] metres of fence is needed.

5 Jamilla is making four curtain poles. She needs three poles that are I m 45 cm and one pole that is 2 m 45 cm. What is the total length of the curtain poles she needs?

Draw a picture to show this. Then solve the problem.

Jamilla needs [ ] m [ ] cm of curtain poles.

6 Which is longer: 5 × 35 cm or 3 × 53 cm? Show your method.

_____ is longer.

7 Ebo cuts these pieces of string in half. Write the missing lengths.

CHALLENGE

a)

3 m

☐ cm

☐ cm

b)

33 cm

☐ cm ☐ mm

☐ cm ☐ mm

c)

1 m 33 cm

☐ cm ☐ mm

☐ cm ☐ mm

Reflect

Susan buys three hose pipes. Each hose pipe is 3 m 60 cm long.
How much hose pipe does she buy?

Tick the **two** calculations you would need to do to solve this problem.

3 + 60 = 63 ☐   9 × 3 = 27 ☐

60 cm × 3 = 180 cm ☐   3 m × 3 = 9 m ☐

Date: _____

End of unit check

My journal

1 Reena and Danny want to know if their combined height is greater than the combined height of Richard and Ambika.

Complete the bar models. Show your working out.

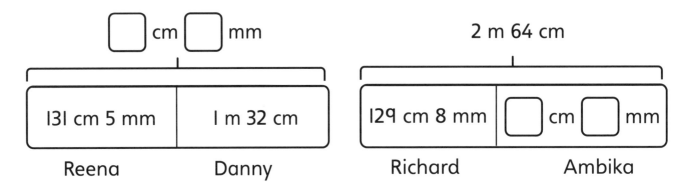

	Reena	Danny
	131 cm 5 mm	1 m 32 cm

Richard	Ambika

⬜ cm ⬜ mm

2 m 64 cm

129 cm 8 mm ⬜ cm ⬜ mm

Work out which pair of children has the greater combined height.

The combined height of _____ and _____

is **greater than** the combined height of _____ and

_____ .

2 Bo measures the perimeter of a rectangular sheet of paper.

30 cm

20 cm

Bo cuts the paper in half. He thinks the perimeter will be halved too.

Is Bo correct? Explain your answer. Use the key words below to help you.

_____

_____

_____

_____

_____

_____

These words might help you.

perimeter   length

centimetre   sides

rectangle   square   width

Power check

How do you feel about your work in this unit?

Power play

A rectangle has a total perimeter of 36 cm. What could the lengths of its sides be?

Find four possible answers.

Length of rectangle	Width of rectangle	Draw what you think it might look like

Try the puzzle again, this time for a rectangle with a total perimeter of 48 cm.

Understand the denominator of unit fractions

1 What fraction of each shape is shaded?

a)

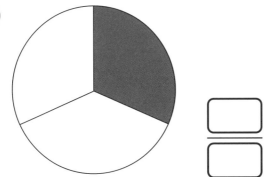

c)

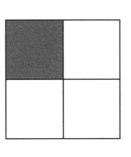

b)

d)

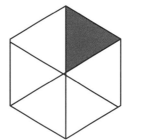

2 What fraction of each shape is shaded?

a)

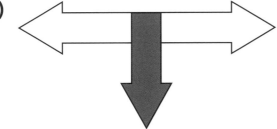

b)

3 **a)** Shade in $\frac{1}{3}$ of each shape.

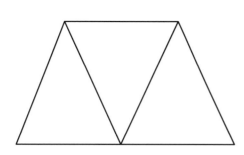 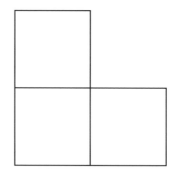

b) Shade in $\frac{1}{8}$ of each shape.

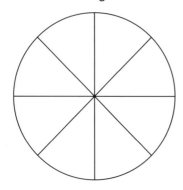 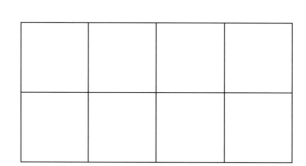

4 Circle all of the unit fractions.

$$\frac{1}{2} \qquad \frac{1}{5} \qquad \frac{2}{4} \qquad \frac{1}{3} \qquad \frac{2}{3} \qquad \frac{1}{9} \qquad \frac{5}{9}$$

5 Shade in $\frac{1}{4}$ of each shape.

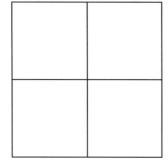 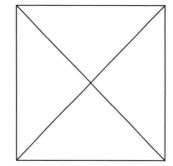 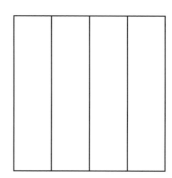

6 Annie says $\frac{1}{4}$ of each shape is shaded.

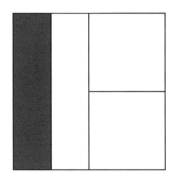 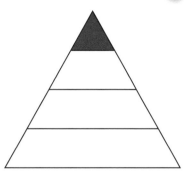

Is Annie correct? Discuss this with a partner.

7 Shade in $\frac{1}{10}$ of this shape.

Reflect

Write down two things you have learnt about unit fractions.

1. _____

_____

2. _____

_____

Date: _____

Compare and order unit fractions

↑ Textbook 3B p116

1 Circle the fraction that is greater.

a)

| $\frac{1}{3}$ | $\frac{1}{3}$ | $\frac{1}{3}$ |

$\frac{1}{3}$

| $\frac{1}{4}$ | $\frac{1}{4}$ | $\frac{1}{4}$ | $\frac{1}{4}$ |

$\frac{1}{4}$

b)

| $\frac{1}{5}$ | $\frac{1}{5}$ | $\frac{1}{5}$ | $\frac{1}{5}$ | $\frac{1}{5}$ |

$\frac{1}{5}$

| $\frac{1}{8}$ | $\frac{1}{8}$ | $\frac{1}{8}$ | $\frac{1}{8}$ | $\frac{1}{8}$ | $\frac{1}{8}$ | $\frac{1}{8}$ | $\frac{1}{8}$ |

$\frac{1}{8}$

2 Circle the fraction that is smaller.

a)

| $\frac{1}{2}$ | $\frac{1}{2}$ |

$\frac{1}{2}$

| $\frac{1}{5}$ | $\frac{1}{5}$ | $\frac{1}{5}$ | $\frac{1}{5}$ | $\frac{1}{5}$ |

$\frac{1}{5}$

b)

| $\frac{1}{6}$ | $\frac{1}{6}$ | $\frac{1}{6}$ | $\frac{1}{6}$ | $\frac{1}{6}$ | $\frac{1}{6}$ |

$\frac{1}{6}$

| $\frac{1}{3}$ | $\frac{1}{3}$ | $\frac{1}{3}$ |

$\frac{1}{3}$

3 Complete the sentences by writing **greater than** or **less than**.

a) $\frac{1}{5}$ is _____ $\frac{1}{3}$.

c) $\frac{1}{5}$ is _____ $\frac{1}{6}$.

b) $\frac{1}{5}$ is _____ $\frac{1}{4}$.

d) $\frac{1}{5}$ is _____ $\frac{1}{10}$.

4 Complete the sentences using < or >.

a) $\frac{1}{4} \bigcirc \frac{1}{5}$

d) $\frac{1}{9} \bigcirc \frac{1}{10}$

b) $\frac{1}{3} \bigcirc \frac{1}{7}$

e) $\frac{1}{10} \bigcirc \frac{1}{20}$

c) $\frac{1}{2} \bigcirc \frac{1}{8}$

f) $\frac{1}{9} \bigcirc \frac{1}{99}$

5 Circle all the fractions less than $\frac{1}{6}$.

$\boxed{\frac{1}{2}}$ $\boxed{\frac{1}{3}}$ $\boxed{\frac{1}{4}}$ $\boxed{\frac{1}{7}}$ $\boxed{\frac{1}{8}}$ $\boxed{\frac{1}{10}}$

6 Write the fractions in order, starting with the smallest.

CHALLENGE

a) $\frac{1}{3}$ $\frac{1}{6}$ $\frac{1}{5}$

_____ , _____ , _____

b) $\frac{1}{5}$ $\frac{1}{8}$ $\frac{1}{2}$ $\frac{1}{12}$

_____ , _____ , _____ , _____

Discuss your method with a partner.

Reflect

Draw diagrams to show that $\frac{1}{3}$ is less than $\frac{1}{2}$.

Understand the numerator of non-unit fractions

1 What fraction of each circle is shaded?

a)

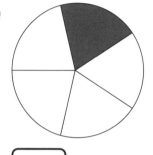

$$\frac{\boxed{}}{\boxed{}}$$

c)

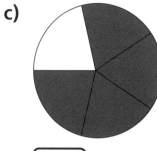

$$\frac{\boxed{}}{\boxed{}}$$

b)

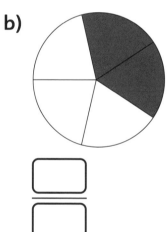

$$\frac{\boxed{}}{\boxed{}}$$

d)

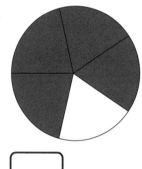

$$\frac{\boxed{}}{\boxed{}}$$

2 What fraction of each shape is shaded?

a)

$$\frac{\boxed{}}{\boxed{}}$$

b)

$$\frac{\boxed{}}{\boxed{}}$$

3 What fraction of each shape is shaded?

a)

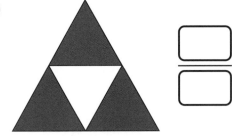

c)

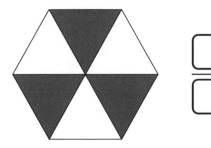

b)

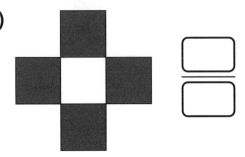

d)

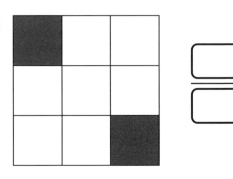

4 Shade in the correct fraction of these circles.

a) $\frac{2}{8}$

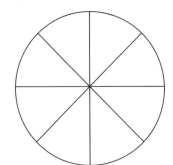

b) $\frac{5}{8}$

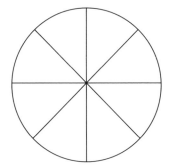

5 $\frac{1}{3}$ of this shape is shaded. Do you agree?

Discuss with a partner.

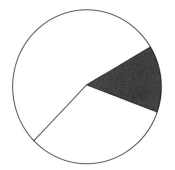

6 a) Shade in $\frac{3}{4}$ of the apples.

b) Shade in $\frac{3}{5}$ of the trees.

c) Shade in $\frac{8}{10}$ of the cats.

7 For the objects on the right, write down

CHALLENGE

a) The fraction that have wheels.

b) The fraction that have four legs.

c) The fraction that are animals.

Reflect

Draw $\frac{2}{3}$ in two different ways.

Date: _____

Understand the whole

1 Use the images to help you complete the fractions.

a)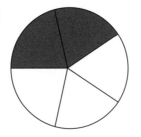
$$\frac{2}{5} + \frac{\boxed{}}{5} = 1$$

b)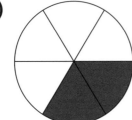
$$\frac{2}{6} + \frac{\boxed{}}{6} = 1$$

c)
$$\frac{5}{8} + \frac{\boxed{}}{8} = 1$$

d)
$$\frac{\boxed{}}{10} + \frac{3}{10} = 1$$

2 Complete the fractions.

a) $\frac{2}{3} + \frac{\boxed{}}{3} = 1$

b) $\frac{6}{7} + \frac{\boxed{}}{7} = 1$

c) $\frac{4}{7} + \frac{\boxed{}}{7} = 1$

d) $\frac{1}{8} + \frac{\boxed{}}{8} = 1$

e) $\frac{5}{10} + \frac{\boxed{}}{10} = 1$

f) $\frac{\boxed{}}{10} + \frac{6}{10} = 1$

3 **a)** The water bottle is $\frac{4}{5}$ full.

What fraction of the bottle is empty?

$$\frac{\boxed{}}{\boxed{}}$$

b) Aki runs $\frac{1}{6}$ of a race.

What fraction of the race does he still have left to run?

$$\frac{\boxed{}}{\boxed{}}$$

4 Find four ways to complete this addition.

$$\frac{\boxed{}}{9} + \frac{\boxed{}}{9} = 1 \qquad\qquad \frac{\boxed{}}{9} + \frac{\boxed{}}{9} = 1$$

$$\frac{\boxed{}}{9} + \frac{\boxed{}}{9} = 1 \qquad\qquad \frac{\boxed{}}{9} + \frac{\boxed{}}{9} = 1$$

5 Explain the mistake in this calculation.

$$\frac{2}{3} + \frac{1}{3} = \frac{3}{6}$$

Can you use the words **numerator** and **denominator** in your answer?

_____

_____

_____

_____

6 Write two different ways that you could share the cake between the 2 plates.

CHALLENGE

I will record each different way as a new calculation.

1 whole cake = $\frac{\square}{\square} + \frac{\square}{\square}$ 1 whole cake = $\frac{\square}{\square} + \frac{\square}{\square}$

Reflect

What did you learn about making the **whole** in this lesson?

I learnt that _____

_____

_____

Compare and order non-unit fractions

→ Textbook 3B p128

1 Circle the fraction that is greater.

a)

$\frac{2}{5}$

$\frac{4}{5}$

b)

$\frac{3}{6}$

$\frac{2}{6}$

2 Circle the fraction that is smaller.

a)
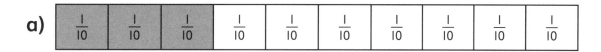

$\frac{3}{10}$

$\frac{8}{10}$

b)

$\frac{7}{8}$

$\frac{5}{8}$

95

3 Complete the sentences by writing **greater than** or **less than**.

a) $\frac{2}{7}$ is _____ $\frac{4}{7}$.

b) $\frac{4}{5}$ is _____ $\frac{1}{5}$.

c) $\frac{7}{9}$ is _____ $\frac{5}{9}$.

d) $\frac{5}{6}$ is _____ I whole.

e) $\frac{7}{10}$ is _____ $\frac{4}{10}$.

4 Complete the sentences using < or >.

a) $\frac{3}{4}$ ◯ $\frac{2}{4}$ d) $\frac{3}{10}$ ◯ $\frac{7}{10}$

b) $\frac{4}{6}$ ◯ $\frac{5}{6}$ e) $\frac{11}{12}$ ◯ $\frac{7}{12}$

c) $\frac{6}{9}$ ◯ $\frac{4}{9}$ f) $\frac{4}{5}$ ◯ I

5 Write the fractions in order, starting with the smallest.

a) $\frac{6}{9}$, $\frac{4}{9}$, $\frac{3}{9}$ b) $\frac{7}{8}$, $\frac{1}{8}$, $\frac{5}{8}$, $\frac{6}{8}$

_____, _____, _____   _____, _____, _____, _____

6 What could the missing numerators be?
Write three answers for each fraction.

a) $\frac{5}{9} > \frac{\boxed{}}{9}$

$\frac{5}{9} > \frac{\boxed{}}{9}$

$\frac{5}{9} > \frac{\boxed{}}{9}$

b) $\frac{2}{6} < \frac{\boxed{}}{6}$

$\frac{2}{6} < \frac{\boxed{}}{6}$

$\frac{2}{6} < \frac{\boxed{}}{6}$

7 Shade in the fraction strips to show that $\frac{5}{6} > \frac{5}{8}$.

CHALLENGE

Reflect

$\frac{\bigcirc}{4} > \frac{\triangle}{4}$

Which is greater, the circle or the triangle? Explain your answer.

_____

_____

_____

Date: _____

Divisions on a number line

1 What fraction does each number line go up in?

Label all the missing fractions.

a)

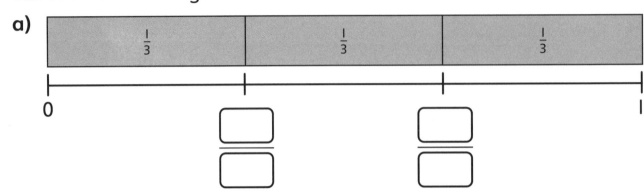

b)

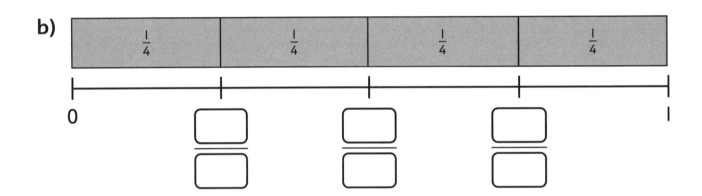

c)

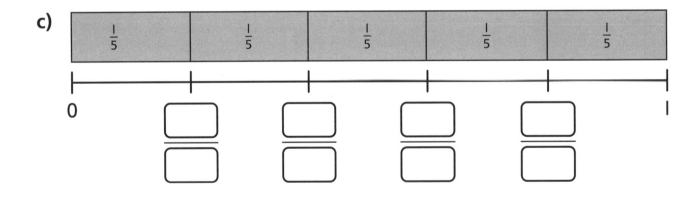

2 Label the missing fractions on the number lines.

a)

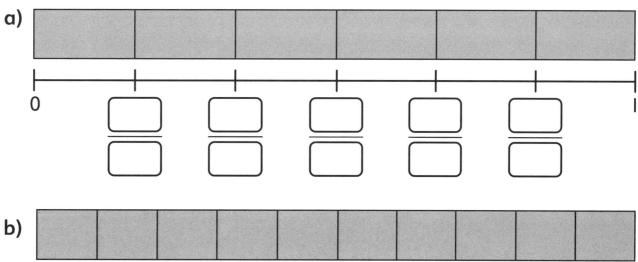

b)

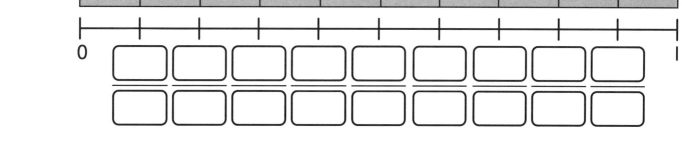

3 What fraction of each jug is full?

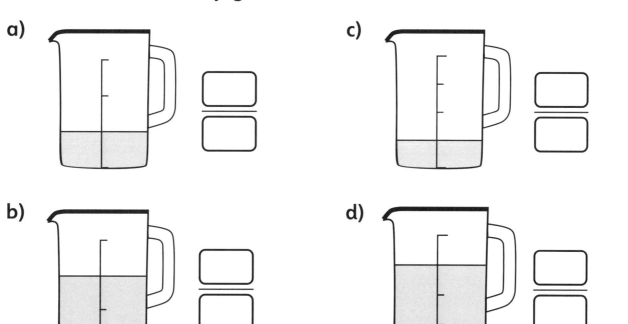

a)

c)

b)

d)

4 Do these number lines go up in quarters? Discuss with a partner.

a)

0   1

b)

0   1

5 a) Mark this line to split it into sixths.

CHALLENGE

0   1

b) Mark this line to split it into eighths.

0   1

Reflect

With a partner, discuss how you can work out what fractions a number line goes up in.

Count in fractions on a number line

Textbook 3B p136

1 Label the fractions on the number lines.

a)
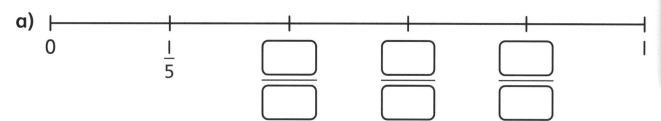

b)
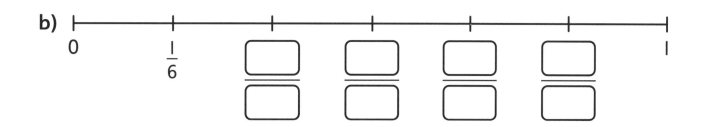

c)
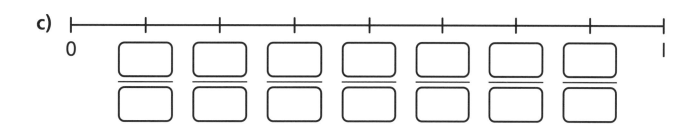

d)
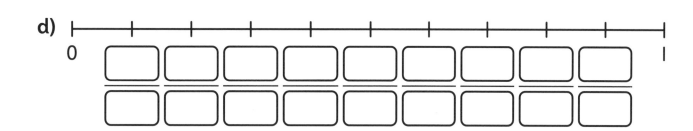

2 Draw arrows to show the correct position of each fraction on the number line.

$\frac{6}{7}$ $\frac{4}{7}$ $\frac{2}{7}$

a)
0

$\frac{5}{9}$ $\frac{1}{9}$ $\frac{9}{9}$ $\frac{7}{9}$

b)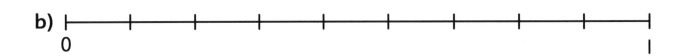
0

3 What fractions are the arrows pointing to?

a)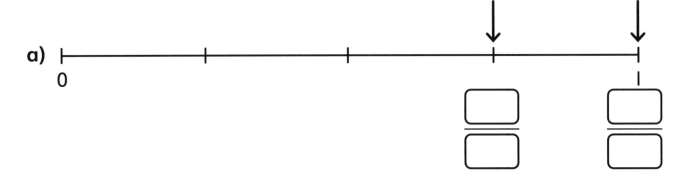
0

b)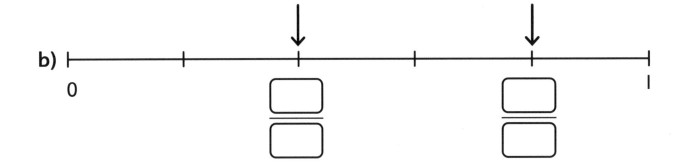
0

4 What fraction of each jug is filled?

a)

b)

5 **a)** Shade in the jug to show it $\frac{3}{8}$ full.

CHALLENGE

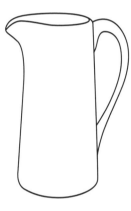

b) A snake is $\frac{7}{10}$ of a metre long.

Draw an estimate to show the length of the snake.

0 m   1 m

Reflect

Draw a number line that you can use with a partner to count up in sixths.

Date: _____

Equivalent fractions as bar models

1 Fill in the missing equivalent fractions.

a) $\dfrac{1}{4} = \dfrac{\boxed{}}{8}$

1			
$\frac{1}{4}$	$\frac{1}{4}$	$\frac{1}{4}$	$\frac{1}{4}$
$\frac{1}{8}$ $\frac{1}{8}$	$\frac{1}{8}$ $\frac{1}{8}$	$\frac{1}{8}$ $\frac{1}{8}$	$\frac{1}{8}$ $\frac{1}{8}$

b) $\dfrac{1}{6} = \dfrac{\boxed{}}{12}$

1					
$\frac{1}{6}$	$\frac{1}{6}$	$\frac{1}{6}$	$\frac{1}{6}$	$\frac{1}{6}$	$\frac{1}{6}$
$\frac{1}{12}$ $\frac{1}{12}$	$\frac{1}{12}$ $\frac{1}{12}$	$\frac{1}{12}$ $\frac{1}{12}$	$\frac{1}{12}$ $\frac{1}{12}$	$\frac{1}{12}$ $\frac{1}{12}$	$\frac{1}{12}$ $\frac{1}{12}$

c) $\dfrac{1}{3} = \dfrac{\boxed{}}{\boxed{}} = \dfrac{\boxed{}}{\boxed{}}$

1		
$\frac{1}{3}$		
$\frac{1}{6}$		
$\frac{1}{12}$		

2 Shade in the fraction strips to show each fraction. Fill in the equivalent fraction.

a) $\dfrac{2}{3} = \dfrac{\boxed{}}{9}$

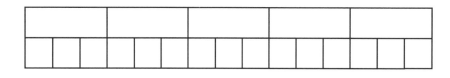

b) $\dfrac{3}{15} = \dfrac{1}{\boxed{}}$

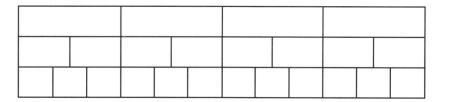

c) $\dfrac{3}{12} = \dfrac{2}{\boxed{}} = \dfrac{\boxed{}}{\boxed{}}$

3 Each fraction matches a fraction strip. Draw lines to match them.

$\dfrac{1}{3}$

$\dfrac{2}{5}$

$\dfrac{1}{4}$

$\dfrac{1}{2}$

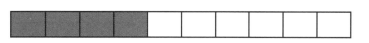

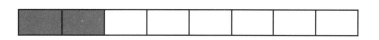

④ Shade $\frac{6}{8}$ in the middle row of the fraction wall. Then shade its equivalent fractions in the top and bottom rows.

Complete the fraction sentence.

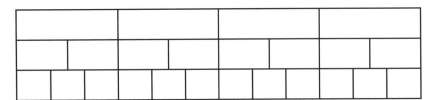

$\frac{6}{8} = \frac{\boxed{}}{\boxed{}} = \frac{\boxed{}}{\boxed{}}$

CHALLENGE

⑤ Olivia has drawn these diagrams. She says that the fractions are equal. Is Olivia correct? Explain your answer.

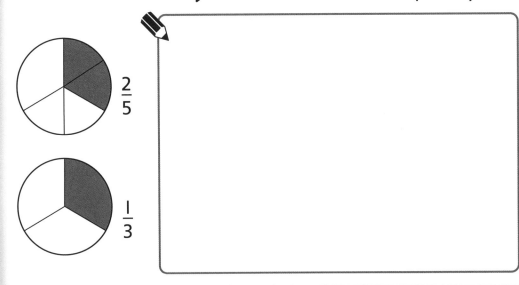

$\frac{2}{5}$

$\frac{1}{3}$

Try drawing a diagram to explain your answer.

Reflect

Explain how you can fold paper to show equivalent fractions.

Date: _____

Equivalent fractions on a number line

1 Use the number lines to work out the equivalent fractions.

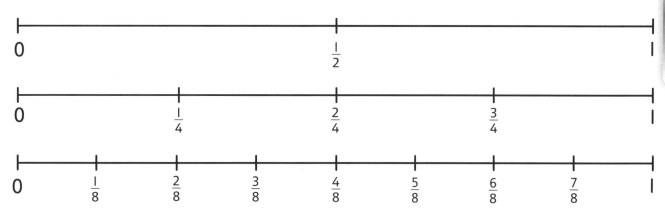

a) $\frac{1}{2} = \dfrac{\boxed{}}{4}$

c) $\frac{3}{4} = \dfrac{\boxed{}}{8}$

b) $\frac{1}{4} = \dfrac{\boxed{}}{8}$

d) $\frac{1}{2} = \dfrac{\boxed{}}{8}$

2 Use the number lines to work out the equivalent fractions.

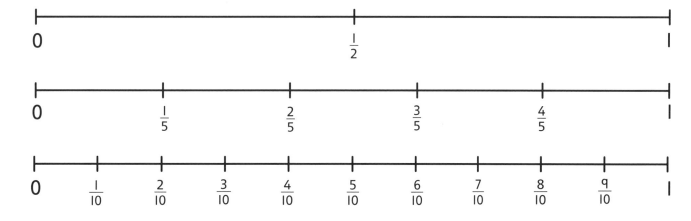

a) $\frac{1}{2} = \dfrac{\boxed{}}{10}$

c) $\frac{2}{5} = \dfrac{\boxed{}}{10}$

b) $\frac{1}{5} = \dfrac{\boxed{}}{10}$

d) $\frac{8}{10} = \dfrac{\boxed{}}{5}$

107

3 Complete the equivalent fractions. Use the number lines to help you.

a) $\dfrac{1}{3} = \dfrac{\boxed{}}{6}$

b) $\dfrac{2}{\boxed{}} = \dfrac{4}{6}$

c) $\dfrac{1}{\boxed{}} = \dfrac{3}{\boxed{}}$

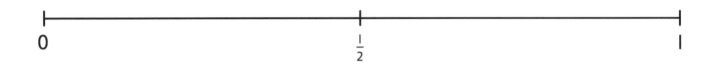

0 ········· $\dfrac{1}{2}$ ········· 1

0 ········· $\dfrac{1}{3}$ ········· 1

0 ····· $\dfrac{1}{6}$ ········· 1

d) Write down three fractions that are **not** equivalent to $\dfrac{1}{3}$.

4 Draw arrows to mark these fractions in the correct positions on the number line.

$\dfrac{1}{2}$ $\dfrac{1}{4}$ $\dfrac{3}{4}$

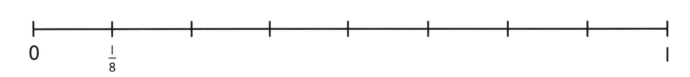

0 ····· $\dfrac{1}{8}$ ········· 1

5 Mark $\frac{1}{3}$ on the top number line. Then circle the fractions on the bottom number line that are **not** equivalent to $\frac{1}{3}$.

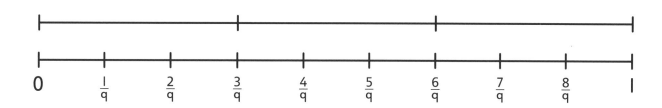

0    $\frac{1}{9}$ $\frac{2}{9}$ $\frac{3}{9}$ $\frac{4}{9}$ $\frac{5}{9}$ $\frac{6}{9}$ $\frac{7}{9}$ $\frac{8}{9}$ 1

6 $\frac{2}{2}$ and $\frac{7}{7}$ are equivalent fractions. How do you know?

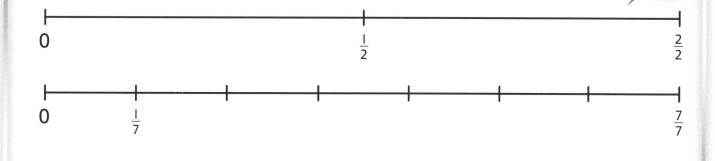

0                    $\frac{1}{2}$ $\frac{2}{2}$

0    $\frac{1}{7}$ $\frac{7}{7}$

_____

_____

Can you find two other fractions equal to $\frac{2}{2}$?

Reflect

Explain how to use number lines to find equivalent fractions.

- _____
- _____
- _____

Date: _____

Equivalent fractions

1 Use the fraction strips and number lines to find the missing numerators.

a) $\dfrac{1}{8} = \dfrac{\boxed{}}{16}$

b) $\dfrac{4}{5} = \dfrac{\boxed{}}{10}$

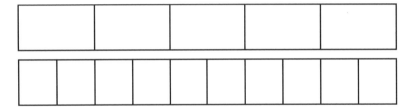

c) $\dfrac{3}{4} = \dfrac{\boxed{}}{12}$

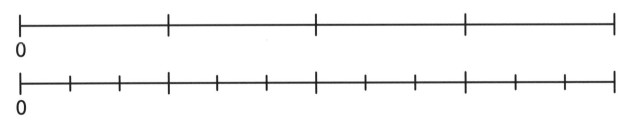

d) $\dfrac{\boxed{}}{4} = \dfrac{12}{16}$

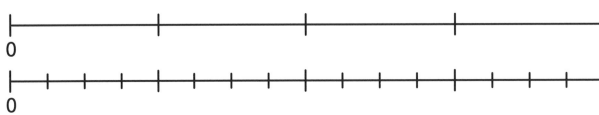

2 **a)** Explain why $\frac{2}{3} = \frac{8}{12}$.

_____

_____

_____

b) Explain why $\frac{2}{5}$ is **not** equal to $\frac{4}{15}$.

_____

_____

_____

3 Complete the missing numbers. Draw lines to join up any equivalent fractions.

a) $\frac{6}{10} = \frac{\boxed{}}{20}$

d) $\frac{\boxed{}}{8} = \frac{1}{2}$

g) $\frac{\boxed{}}{32} = \frac{1}{8}$

b) $\frac{3}{4} = \frac{\boxed{}}{16}$

e) $\frac{5}{11} = \frac{30}{\boxed{}}$

h) $\frac{\boxed{}}{36} = \frac{3}{9}$

c) $\frac{8}{12} = \frac{\boxed{}}{6}$

f) $\frac{5}{\boxed{}} = \frac{1}{3}$

i) $\frac{5}{7} = \frac{\boxed{}}{28}$

I wonder if I should multiply or divide to find the missing numbers.

4 The is a number between 35 and 45.

What pairs of numbers could the ⬤ and ▲ be?

$$\frac{3}{4} = \frac{\bigcirc}{\triangle}$$

---

5 Emma thinks that $\frac{1}{2}$ is equivalent to $\frac{2}{3}$.

This is how she worked out her answer.

Do you agree with Emma? Explain how you know.

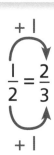

_____

_____

_____

Reflect

Explain why $\frac{4}{10}$ is equivalent to $\frac{2}{5}$.

_____

_____

End of unit check

My journal

What can you say about the value of the circle compared with the value of the square?

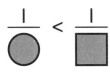

$\dfrac{1}{\bigcirc} < \dfrac{1}{\square}$

_____

_____

_____

_____

What can you say about the value of the triangle compared with the value of the pentagon?

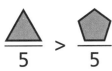

$\dfrac{\triangle}{5} > \dfrac{\pentagon}{5}$

_____

_____

_____

_____

Power check

How do you feel about your work in this unit?

Power puzzle

Shade in $\frac{1}{2}$ of each grid.

Shade $\frac{1}{2}$ in different ways.

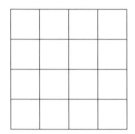 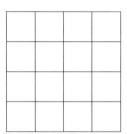 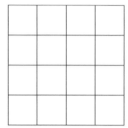

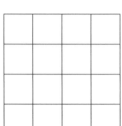 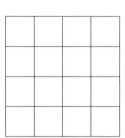 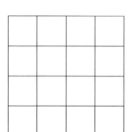

I like to make different patterns.

Shade in $\frac{1}{3}$ of each grid.

Shade $\frac{1}{3}$ in different ways.

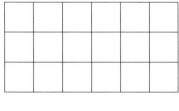 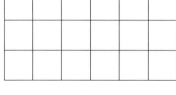 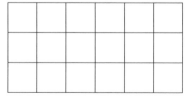

 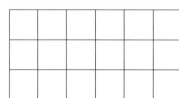 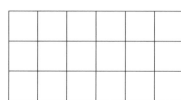

Use scales

→ Textbook 3B p156

1 Complete the number lines.

a)

b)

c)
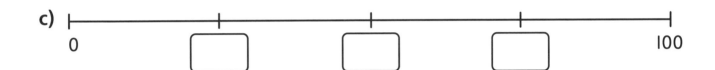

2

This number line goes up in 25s.

Emma

Is Emma correct? Explain your answer.

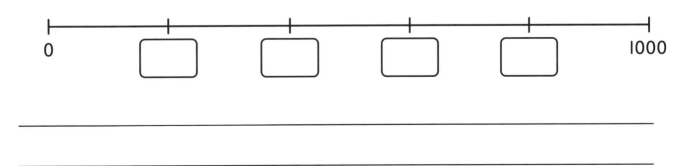

_____

_____

3 Complete the number lines.

a)

0 ▢ ▢ ▢ ▢ ▢ ▢ ▢ ▢ ▢ 1,000

b)

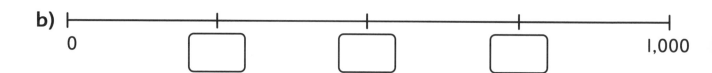

0 ▢ ▢ ▢ 1,000

4 Label all the markings on the scales.

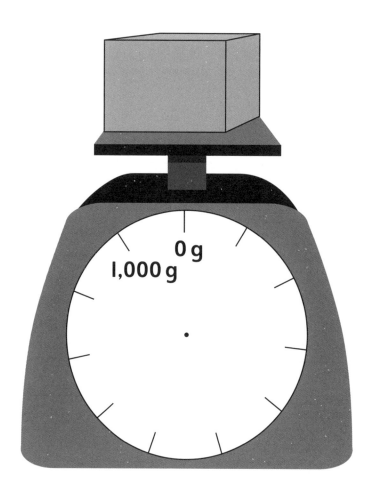

5 What numbers are the arrows pointing to?

a)

0   ↑   ↑   ↑500

This number line goes up in steps of ☐.

b)

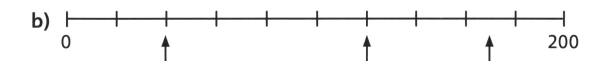
0   ↑   ↑   ↑   200

This number line goes up in steps of ☐.

c)

0   ↑   ↑   500

This number line goes up in steps of ☐.

Reflect

To work out what steps a number line goes up in, I will _____

_____

_____

_____

Date: _____

Measure mass

1 Draw the pointer in the correct place on each measuring scale.

a)

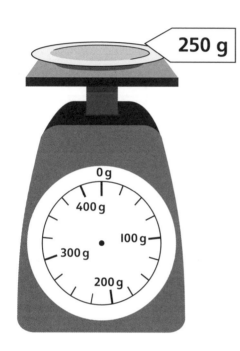
250 g

c)

750 g

b)

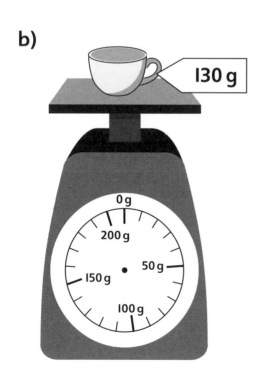
130 g

d)

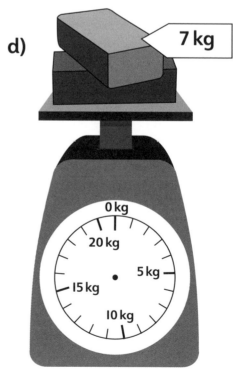
7 kg

2 What is the mass of each of these objects?

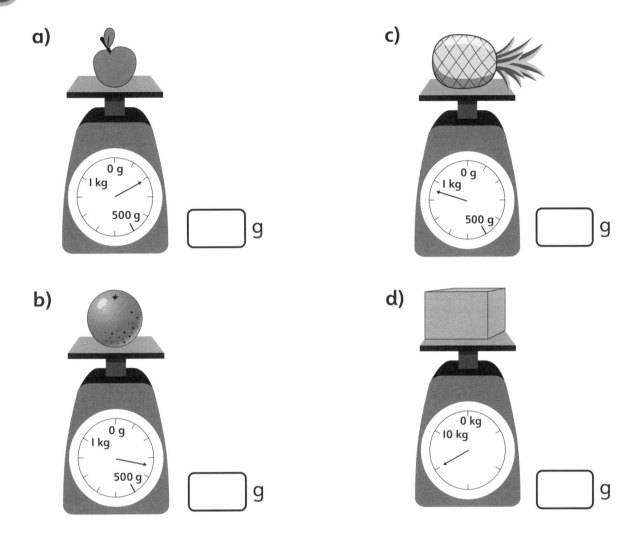

a)

☐ g

b)

☐ g

c)

☐ g

d)

☐ g

3 Andy thinks that the scale shows a mass of 250 g. Do you agree?

Discuss with a partner.

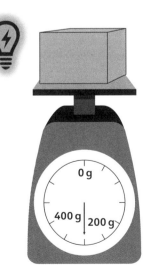

4 Circle the most sensible unit of measure for each object.

g kg   g kg

g kg   g kg

5 Look at the two scales. There are no units marked.
Why could Object 2 have a greater mass than Object 1?

CHALLENGE

Object 1   Object 2

0
600   0   2

I will use my knowledge of grams and kilograms.

The second object could weigh more because _____

_____

_____

Reflect

List some objects in your classroom whose masses you would measure
in kilograms and some you would measure in grams.

Measure mass in kilograms and grams

→ Textbook 3B p164

1 What is the mass of each box?

a)

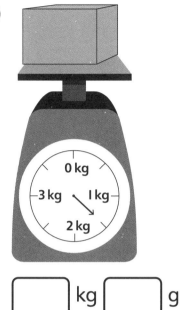

[ ] kg [ ] g

c)

[ ] kg [ ] g

b)

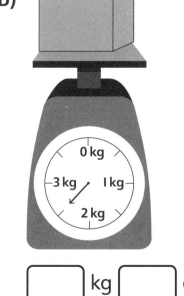

[ ] kg [ ] g

d)

[ ] kg [ ] g

2 Draw a pointer showing the correct mass on each scale.

a)

3 kg 500 g

0 kg
5 kg   1 kg
4 kg   2 kg
3 kg

b)

1 kg 250 g

0 kg
5 kg

3 What mass does each scale show?

a)

0 g
2 kg
500 g
1 kg
500 g   1 kg

[ ] kg [ ] g

c)

0 g
2 kg
500 g
1 kg
500 g   1 kg

[ ] kg [ ] g

b)

0 g
2 kg
500 g
1 kg
500 g   1 kg

[ ] kg [ ] g

d)

0 g
2 kg
1 kg

[ ] kg [ ] g

4 Draw lines to match the amounts to the scale readings.

| 2 kg 100 g | 2 kg 50 g | 2 kg 125 g |

5 Tom measures the mass of some objects.

Estimate the mass of each object.

CHALLENGE

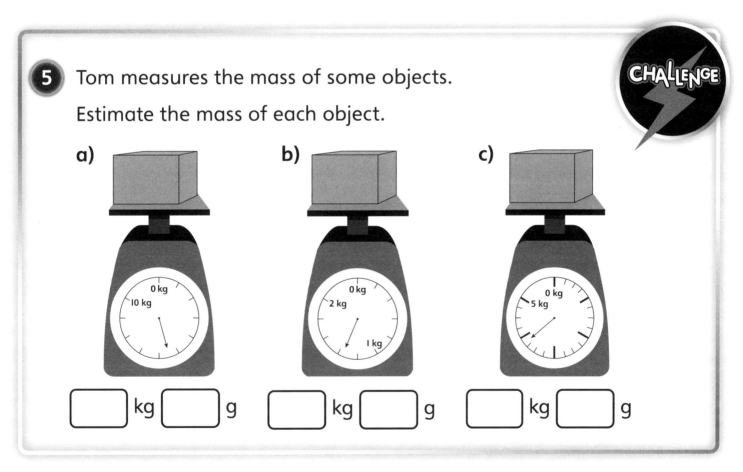

a)

☐ kg ☐ g

b)

☐ kg ☐ g

c)

☐ kg ☐ g

Reflect

Which scales did you find most challenging to read?

Discuss it with a partner and share tips to help each other.

Date: _____

Equivalent masses

1 Complete the part-whole models.

a)

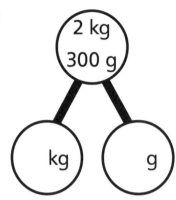

c)

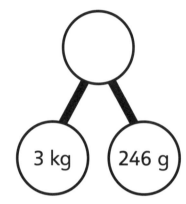

b)

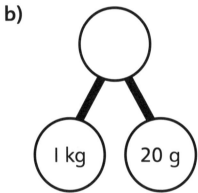

d)

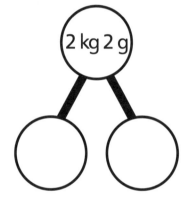

2 Complete the table.

Mass in kilograms and grams	Mass in grams
1 kg	
$\frac{1}{2}$ kg	
$\frac{1}{4}$ kg	

3 Circle the weights to make each mass.

a) 2 kg 600 g

b) 3 kg 200 g

4 Read the scales and write each mass in kilograms and grams.

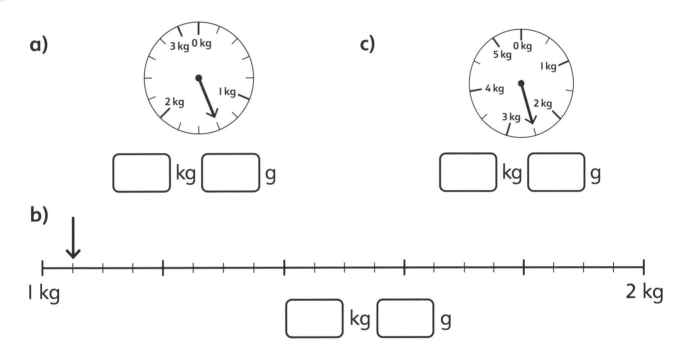

a)

[ ] kg [ ] g

c)

[ ] kg [ ] g

b)

1 kg   2 kg

[ ] kg [ ] g

5 Is Lee correct? Explain why.

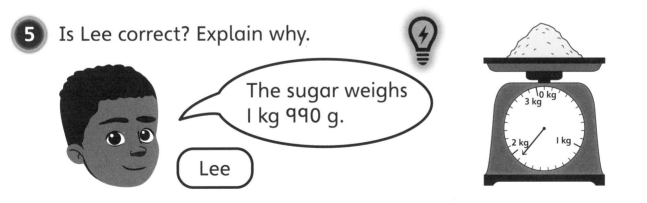

The sugar weighs 1 kg 990 g.

Lee

Lee is correct / incorrect because _____

_____

_____

6 How many different ways can you balance 2 kg 750 g using the weights? You can use the same weight more than once in each way that you balance the scales. Draw your answers below.

CHALLENGE

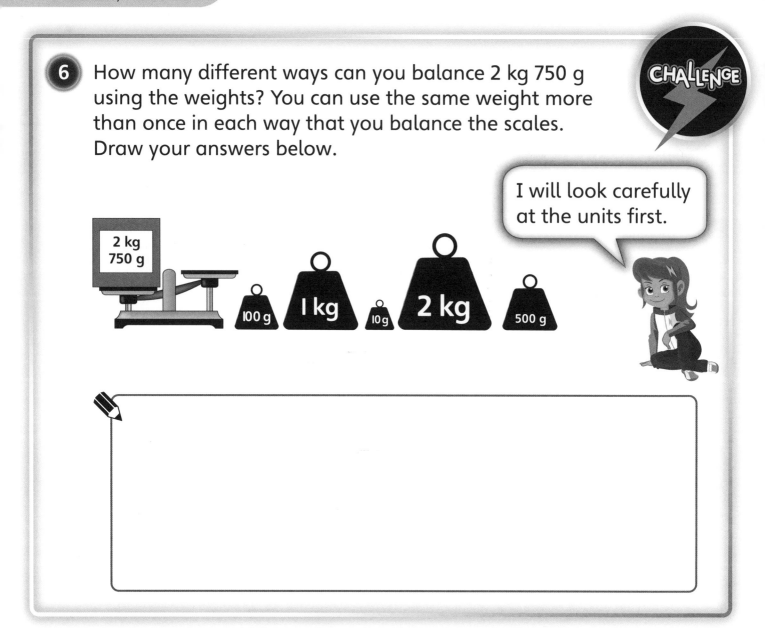

I will look carefully at the units first.

Reflect

Describe some real-life situations where it would be better to record the mass of things using grams and when it would be better to use kilograms.

Compare mass

1 Tick the heavier object in each pair.

a)

450 g   350 g

☐   ☐

b)

7 kg   55 kg

☐   ☐

c)

3 kg 20 g   1 kg 700 g

☐   ☐

d)

1 kg 300 g   1 kg 750 g

☐   ☐

2 Tick the lighter object in each pair.

a)

185 g   90 g

☐   ☐

c)

700 g   2 kg

☐   ☐

b)

1 kg 700 g   2 kg 150 g

☐   ☐

3 Use <, > and = to compare these amounts.

a) 2 kg ◯ 300 kg

b) 2 kg ◯ 500 g

c) 2 kg 10 g ◯ 2 kg 620 g

d) 883 g ◯ 3 kg 180 g

4 Circle the scale that shows the lightest mass of nuts.

a)

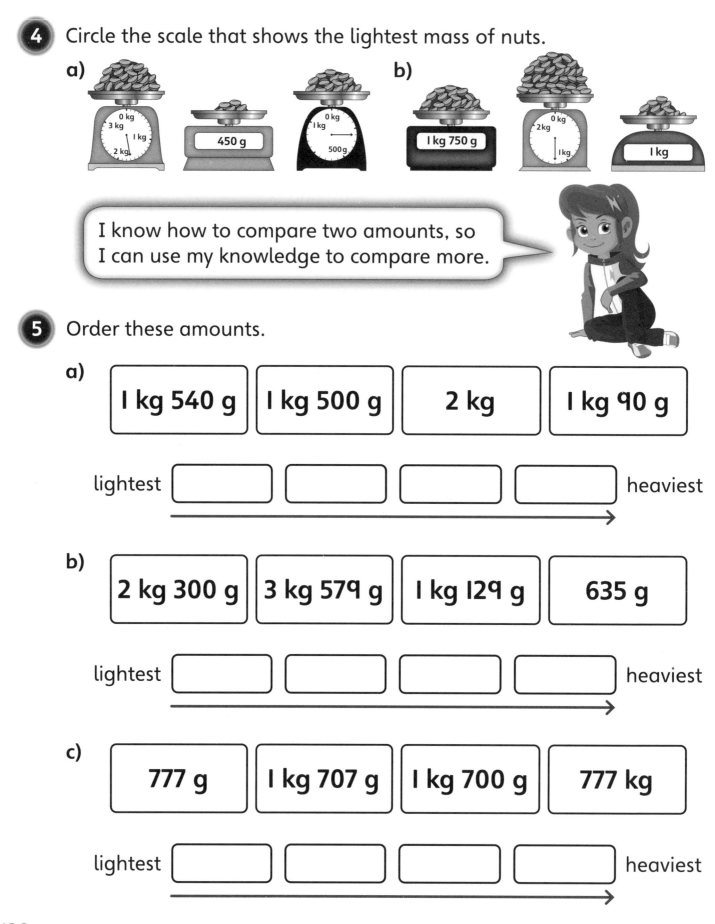

0 kg
3 kg
1 kg
2 kg

450 g

0 kg
1 kg
500 g

b)

1 kg 750 g

0 kg
2 kg
1 kg

1 kg

> I know how to compare two amounts, so I can use my knowledge to compare more.

5 Order these amounts.

a)

| 1 kg 540 g | 1 kg 500 g | 2 kg | 1 kg 90 g |

lightest ☐ ☐ ☐ ☐ heaviest

b)

| 2 kg 300 g | 3 kg 579 g | 1 kg 129 g | 635 g |

lightest ☐ ☐ ☐ ☐ heaviest

c)

| 777 g | 1 kg 707 g | 1 kg 700 g | 777 kg |

lightest ☐ ☐ ☐ ☐ heaviest

6 A is heavier than B. C is heavier than A. D is lighter than B.

A  B 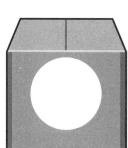 C 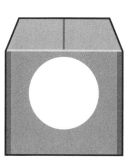 D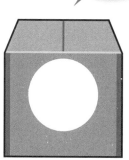

1 kg 20 g

What could the masses of B, C and D be?

B = [ ]   C = [ ]   D = [ ]

Reflect

Max has 1 kg 265 g of coconuts and 2 kg of plums. How could Max know that the plums have a greater mass?

_____

_____

_____

Date: _____

Add and subtract mass

1 Find the total mass of each pair of boxes.

a)

The total mass is ☐.

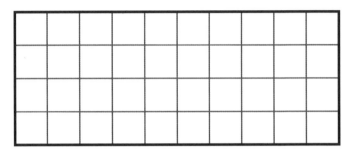

b)

The total mass is ☐.

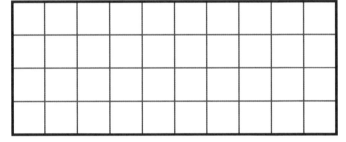

c)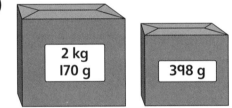

The total mass is ☐.

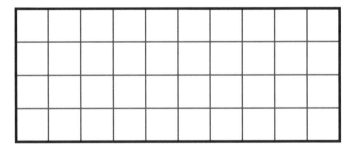

d)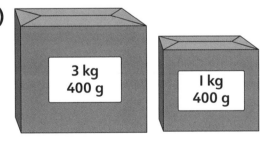

The total mass is ☐.

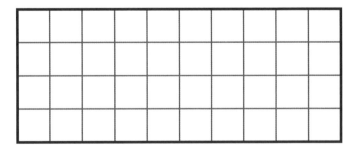

2 Complete the number lines.

a)

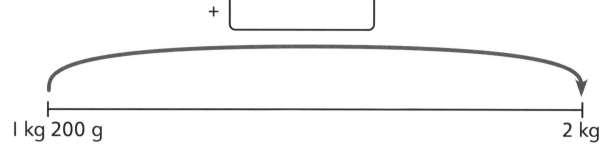

+ [ ]

1 kg 200 g   2 kg

b)

+ 500 g

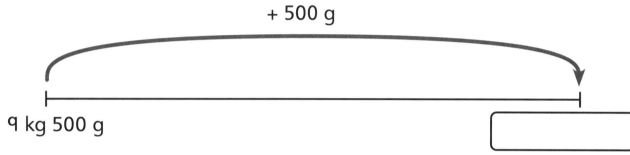

9 kg 500 g

[ ]

3 Complete the bar models.

a)

1 kg 200 g	600 g

c)

1 kg 100 g

b)

1 kg 300 g
900 g	

d)

1 kg 750 g
	310 g

4 Work out the following subtractions.

a) 5 kg 700 g – 1 kg 380 g = [ ] kg [ ] g

b) 3 kg 700 g – 356 g = [ ] kg [ ] g

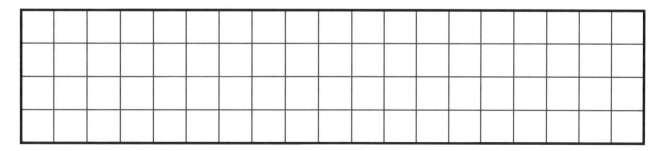

5 Complete the missing numbers.

a) 300 g + ☐ = 1 kg 200 g

b) ☐ + 1 kg 300 g = 1 kg 850 g

c) 1 kg 100 g − ☐ = 20 g

d) ☐ − 1 kg 310 g = 1 kg 400 g

> I will check my answers using an inverse operation.

Reflect

Describe one method you can use to add masses with mixed units.

To add measures with mixed units, I _____

_____

_____

↓ Textbook 3B p180

Problem solving – mass

 a) Alex has 400 g of baking powder. She puts 250 g back on the shelf. How much does she have left?

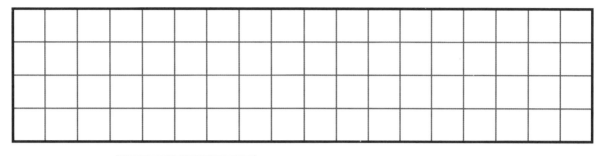

Alex has [   ] left.

b) Zac has 300 g of spices. Mia has 498 g of spices. How much do they have altogether?

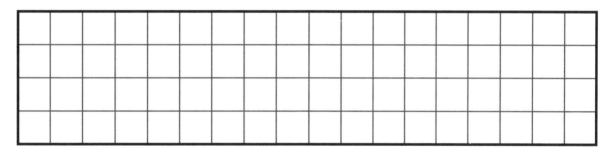

They have [   ] altogether.

c) Zac buys 300 g more flour than Alex. Alex buys 150 g of flour. How much do they buy in total?

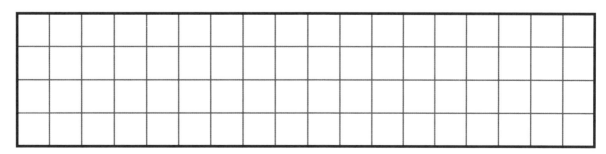

They buy [   ] in total.

2 Work out the mass of the nuts in this recipe.

45 g flour
65 g sugar
200 g butter
? nuts
Total mass: 750 g

The nuts weigh ☐ g.

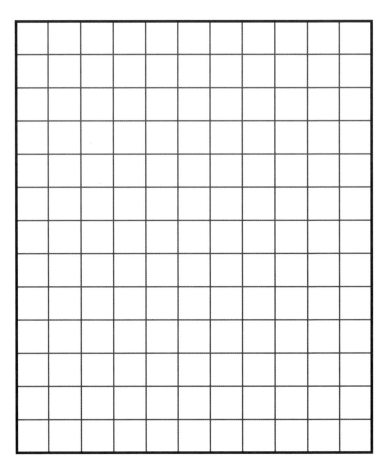

3 Jamilla has three guinea pigs.

The youngest weighs 500 g and the oldest weighs 800 g.
In total, all three weigh 2 kg.

How much does the middle guinea pig weigh?

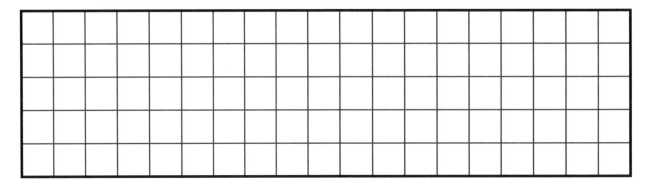

The middle guinea pig weighs ☐ g.

4 What is the mass of the heart?

I remember what I did when I came across a similar problem before.

CHALLENGE

Reflect

The answer to a question is 550 g. What could the question be?

- _____
- _____
- _____

Date: _____

End of unit check

My journal

↑ Textbook 3B p184

Complete the table.

Objects you would measure mass in kg	Objects you would measure mass in g

Circle the objects you think are heaviest and lightest.

Power check

How do you feel about your work in this unit?

Power puzzle

Explain how to calculate the mass of the melon.

Date: _____

Measure capacity and volume in litres and millilitres

> I wonder what each interval is worth.

1 How much liquid is there in each container?

a) 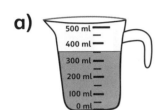  ml

b) 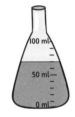 ml

c)  ml

d) 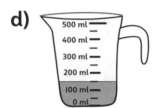 ml

e)  ml

f) 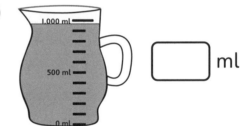 ml

2 Which measure of capacity would you use? Write millilitres or litres under each item.

a)

_____

b)

_____

c)

_____

3 How much water is in each container?

a)
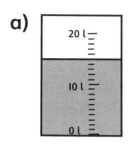

☐ l

b)
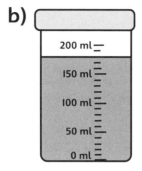

☐ ml

c)
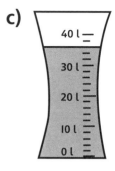

☐ l

4 Draw the arrow on each fuel gauge so that it points to 40 l.

a)
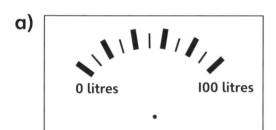

c)
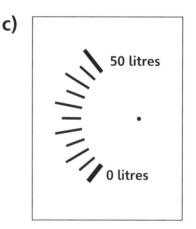

b)
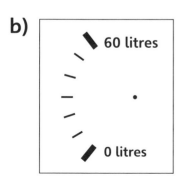

d)
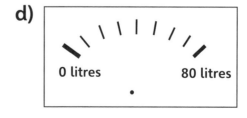

Look carefully at the numbers on each scale.

5 How can you divide the scales evenly so that you can measure 100 ml?

Draw the scale and mark where 100 ml goes.

CHALLENGE

200 ml

0 ml

1 l

0 l

500 ml

0 ml

I will need a ruler for this.

Reflect

To work out how much liquid is in a measuring jug, I need to _____

_____

_____

Date: _____

Measure in litres and millilitres

1 How much liquid is in each jug?

→ Textbook 3B p192

a)

[ ] l [ ] ml

b)

[ ] l [ ] ml

c)

[ ] l [ ] ml

d)

[ ] l [ ] ml

e)

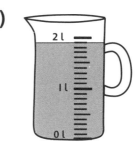

[ ] l [ ] ml

f)

[ ] l [ ] ml

2 Colour in the correct amount of liquid in each measuring jug.

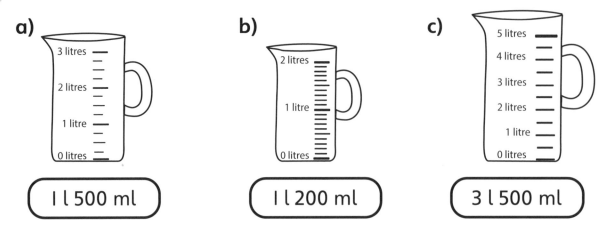

a)

I l 500 ml

b)

I l 200 ml

c)

3 l 500 ml

3 Draw the arrow in the correct place on each fuel gauge.

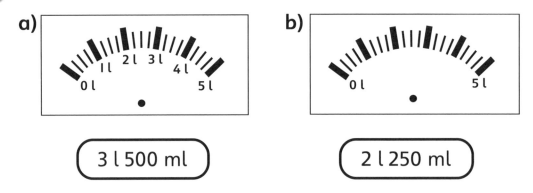

a)

3 l 500 ml

b)

2 l 250 ml

4 The large jug was empty. Then one smaller full jug was tipped into it. Which smaller jug was used?

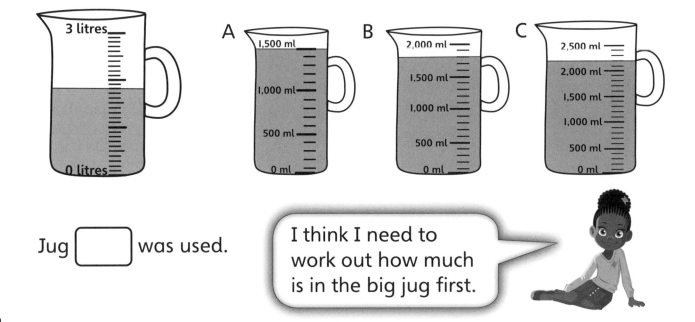

Jug [ ] was used.

I think I need to work out how much is in the big jug first.

5 Approximately how much is in the jug?

I think ☐ l ☐ ml is a good estimate because

_____

_____

_____

Reflect

Draw two measuring scales to show 1 l split into four intervals and five intervals.

Show the different labels for each.

Date: _____

Equivalent capacities and volumes (litres and millilitres)

1 **a)** What is $\frac{1}{2}$ litre in ml?

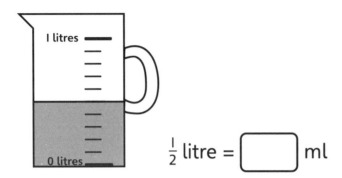

$\frac{1}{2}$ litre = ☐ ml

b) Complete the bar model to write $\frac{1}{4}$ litre in millilitres.

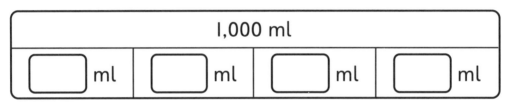

$\frac{1}{4}$ litre = ☐ ml

2 Draw a model to work out $\frac{1}{10}$ of a litre.

3 A carton of milk contains I litre.

a) How many 100 ml glasses can be poured from the carton of milk?

b) How many 50 ml glasses can be poured from the carton of milk?

4 How much water is in each jug?

a)

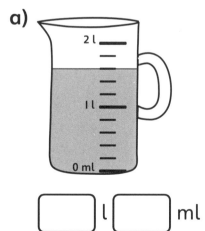

☐ l ☐ ml

b)

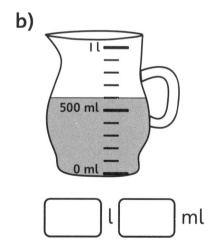

☐ l ☐ ml

5 Mark out each measure on the measuring jug.

a) $1\frac{1}{2}$ litres

b) $1\frac{1}{4}$ litre

6 A recipe needs $\frac{3}{5}$ litre of tomato juice.

How much tomato juice is needed?

Reflect

What fractions of a litre do you know?

Date: _____

Compare capacity and volume

1 Circle the bottle with the greater capacity in each pair.

a)
330 ml | 750 ml

b)
2 l | 3 l

c)
1 l 400 ml | 1 l 650 ml

d)
1 l | 999 ml

e)
1 l 300 ml | 3 l 700 ml

f)
2 l | 375 ml

2 Write these amounts in order, from smallest to greatest.

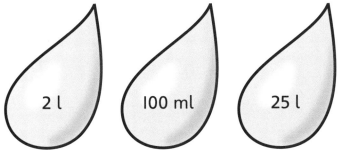

2 l | 100 ml | 25 l

Smallest ⟶ Greatest

I will need to check carefully. There are litres and millilitres.

147

3 Order the containers from smallest capacity to greatest.

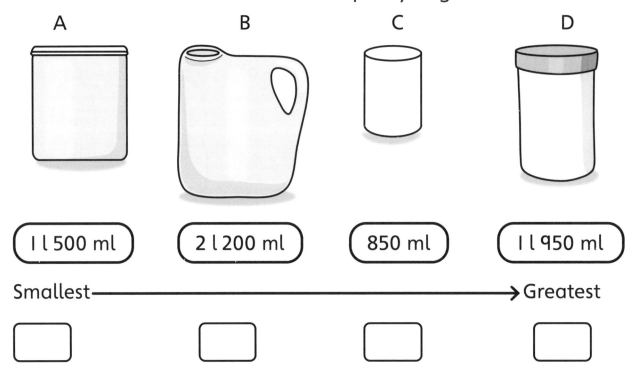

A   B   C   D

(1 l 500 ml)   (2 l 200 ml)   (850 ml)   (1 l 950 ml)

Smallest ⟶ Greatest

4 Look at the amounts shown by the arrows. Put them in order, from the smallest to the greatest amount.

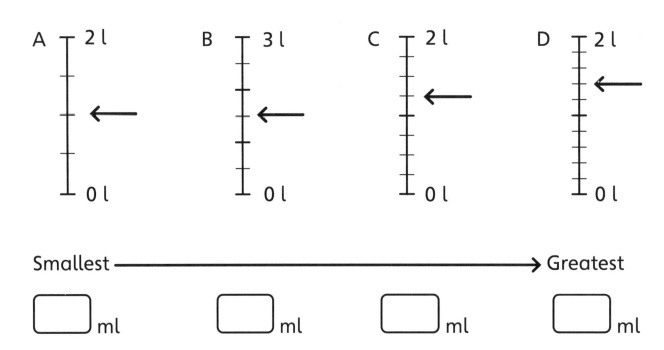

A   2 l   B   3 l   C   2 l   D   2 l

0 l   0 l   0 l   0 l

Smallest ⟶ Greatest

ml   ml   ml   ml

5 Jessica needs a mixing bowl. It should hold less than $2\frac{1}{2}$ l, but more than $1\frac{1}{4}$ l. Which one should she choose?

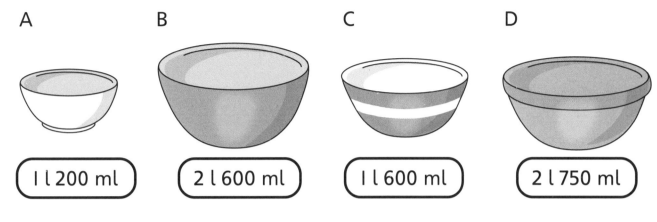

A   1 l 200 ml

B   2 l 600 ml

C   1 l 600 ml

D   2 l 750 ml

Jessica should choose bowl _____.

6 Which container has more liquid in it?
Explain your reasoning.

CHALLENGE

_____

_____

_____

_____

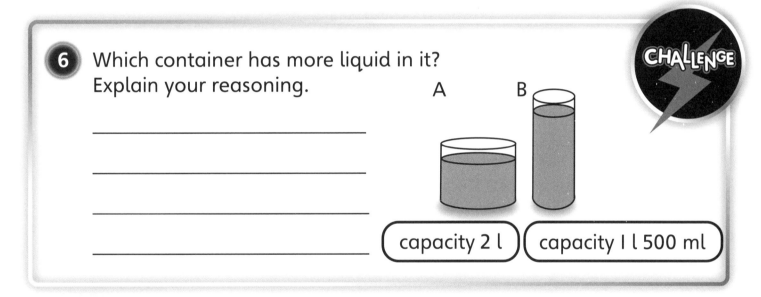

A   capacity 2 l

B   capacity 1 l 500 ml

Reflect

How do you know that 1 litre is greater than 750 ml?

- _____
- _____
- _____

Date: _____

Add and subtract capacity and volume

1 **a)** What is the total of these two amounts?

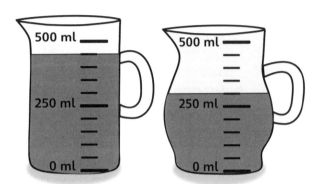

		H	T	O	
		4	5	0	
	+	3	0	0	

b) What is the total of these two amounts?

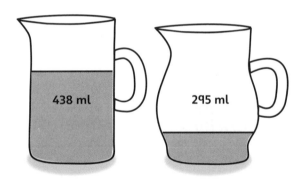
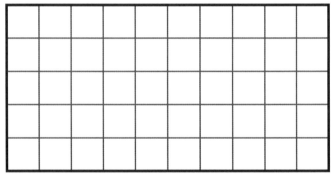

c) What is the total of 3 l 250 ml + 2 l 425 ml?

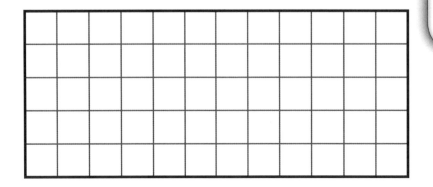

I will try adding the litres and millilitres separately.

2 The cup has been filled from the bottle. How much liquid is left in the bottle?

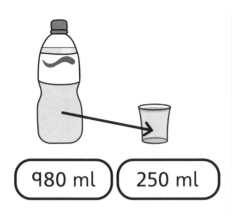

980 ml   250 ml

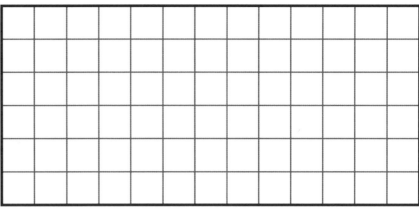

3 How much will be left in the large container?

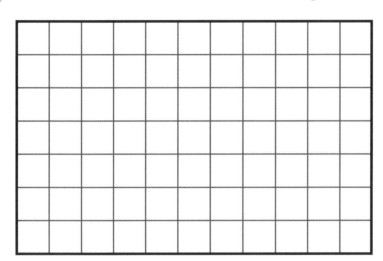

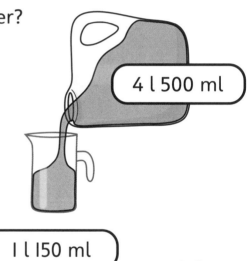

4 l 500 ml

1 l 150 ml

4 James has 2 jugs of water.

Each jug contains 750 ml.

How much water does he have in total?

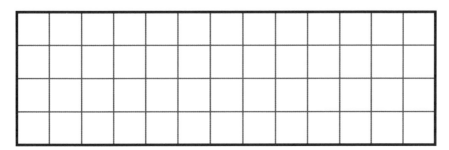

I will work out what I need to make 1 litre first.

151

5 The liquid in the three cylinders exactly fills the 2 l jug. How much is in cylinder C?

CHALLENGE

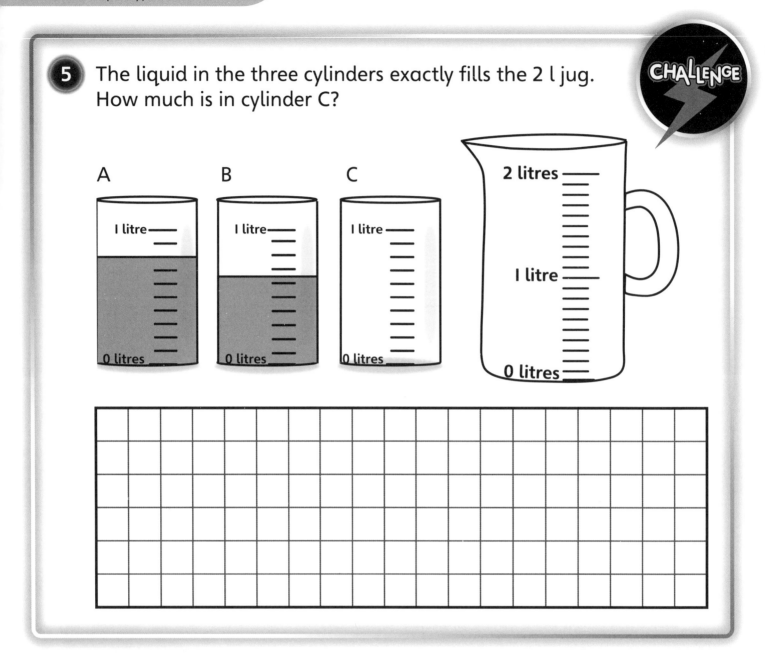

Reflect

Explain how to add together 2 l 800 ml and 1,250 ml.

Date: _____

Problem solving – capacity

1 Paolo bought four bottles of water. Each bottle contained 200 ml.
How much water did he buy altogether?

200 ml	200 ml	200 ml	200 ml

☐ ml

Paolo bought ☐ ml of water altogether.

2 Maria has a 12 l bucket of water. She can fill three smaller buckets.
Each smaller bucket holds the same amount of water.
How many l does each small bucket hold?

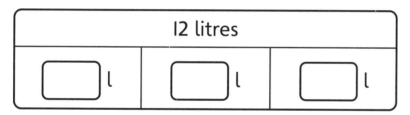

Each small bucket holds ☐ l of water.

3 Frederica puts 40 l of fuel in her car. She uses $\frac{1}{4}$ of the fuel.
How much does she have left?

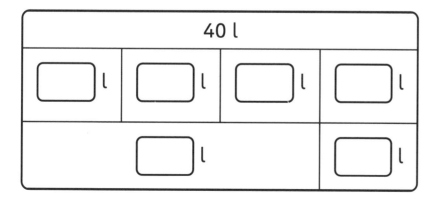

To find $\frac{1}{4}$ of a
number, divide by 4.

Frederica has ☐ l of fuel left.

153

4 A cook uses $\frac{1}{2}$ l plus one 250 ml carton of milk.
How much milk is that in total?

The total is ☐ ml.

5 Alfredo and Jen each like to drink 2 l of water a day. Alfredo uses a 250 ml glass and Jen uses a 200 ml glass. How many glasses of water does each person need to drink each day?

Alfredo needs to drink ☐ glasses.

Jen needs to drink ☐ glasses.

6 A chef needs 800 ml of cream for his recipe. He has three cartons of cream with 50 ml in each. How much more cream does he need?

He needs ☐ ml more cream.

7 A tomato plant needs 500 ml of water a day.

CHALLENGE

a) How much water will you need to water the plant for 7 days?

You will need ☐ l ☐ ml.

b) How much will you need to water 3 plants for 7 days?

You will need ☐ l ☐ ml.

Reflect

Explain how you worked out the answer to a question that needed more than one calculation.

Date: _____

End of unit check

My journal

1. Use the bar models to work out

   a) $\frac{1}{4}$ litre in ml = [ ] ml

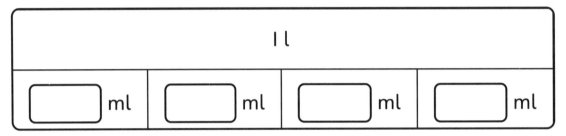

   b) $\frac{3}{4}$ of a litre = [ ] l

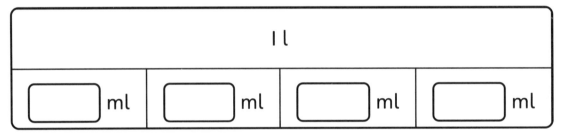

   c) $\frac{4}{5}$ of $\frac{1}{2}$ litre = [ ] l

Power check

How do you feel about your work in this unit?

Power play

This is a game to play with a partner. You need a dice and two counters.

One of you will add millilitres and the other will subtract millilitres.

To start the game, place your counters at 2 l on the scale below.

Take turns to roll a dice.

Scores:

l: + or – **1**00 ml   2: + or – **2**00 ml   3: + or – **3**00 ml

4: + or – **4**00 ml   5: + or – **5**00 ml   6: + or – **6**00 ml

The first person to reach 4 l (adding) or 0 l (subtracting) wins.

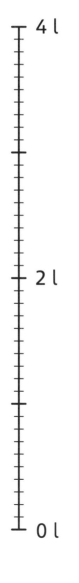

Can you make this game more challenging by drawing a different scale?

My power points

Colour the ☆ next to the topics you have done.

Colour the ☺ when you feel confident about the topic.

Unit 6

I can …

☆ ☺ Recognise multiples of 10

☆ ☺ Multiply 2-digit numbers by 1-digit numbers

☆ ☺ Use known multiplication facts to solve division problems

☆ ☺ Find multiplication and division fact families

☆ ☺ Multiply and divide by partitioning

☆ ☺ Solve multiplication and division problems including multi-step problems

Unit 7

I can …

☆ ☺ Measure lengths in millimetres, centimetres and metres

☆ ☺ Understand equivalent lengths

☆ ☺ Compare lengths

☆ ☺ Add and subtract lengths

☆ ☺ Calculate the perimeter of a shape

Unit 8

I can …

⭐ ☺ Understand denominators and numerators

⭐ ☺ Compare and order fractions

⭐ ☺ Understand the whole

⭐ ☺ Count in fractions on a number line

⭐ ☺ Find equivalent fractions

Unit 9

I can …

⭐ ☺ Work out different intervals on a scale

⭐ ☺ Measure mass in kilograms and grams

⭐ ☺ Add, subtract and compare masses

⭐ ☺ Solve problems involving mass

Unit 10

I can …

⭐ ☺ Measure capacity and volume in litres and millilitres

⭐ ☺ Understand equivalent capacities

⭐ ☺ Compare capacity and volume

⭐ ☺ Add and subtract capacities and volumes

⭐ ☺ Solve problems involving capacity

Keep up the good work!

Published by Pearson Education Limited, 80 Strand, London, WC2R 0RL.

www.pearsonschools.co.uk

Text © Pearson Education Limited 2018, 2022
Edited by Pearson and Florence Production Ltd
First edition edited by Pearson, Little Grey Cells Publishing Services and Haremi Ltd
Designed and typeset by Pearson, Florence Production Ltd and PDQ Digital Media Solutions Ltd
First edition designed and typeset by Kamae Design
Original illustrations © Pearson Education Limited 2017, 2022
Illustrated by Laura Arias, Fran and David Brylewski, Diego Diaz, Nigel Dobbyn and Nadene Naude at
Beehive Illustration, Kamae Design, Florence Production Ltd, and PDQ Digital Media Solutions Ltd
Images: The Royal Mint, 1971, 1990, 1992: 10, 53
Cover design by Pearson Education Ltd
Front and back cover illustrations by Diego Diaz and Nadene Naude at Beehive Illustration

Series Editor: Tony Staneff
Lead author: Josh Lury
Authors (first edition): Tony Staneff, David Board, Belle Cottingham, Jonathan East, Tim Handley, Derek Huby,
Neil Jarrett and Timothy Weal
Consultants (first edition): Professor Liu Jian and Professor Zhang Dan

The rights of Tony Staneff and Josh Lury to be identified as authors of this work have been asserted by them in
accordance with the Copyright, Designs and Patents Act 1988.

This publication is protected by copyright, and permission should be obtained from the publisher prior to any prohibited
reproduction, storage in a retrieval system, or transmission in any form or by any means, electronic, mechanical,
photocopying, recording, or otherwise. For information regarding permissions, request forms and the appropriate
contacts, please visit https://www.pearson.com/us/contact-us/permissions.html Pearson Education Limited Rights and
Permissions Department.

First published 2018
This edition first published 2022

25
10 9 8

British Library Cataloguing in Publication Data
A catalogue record for this book is available from the British Library

ISBN 978 1 292 41943 5

Copyright notice
All rights reserved. No part of this publication may be reproduced in any form or by any means (including
photocopying or storing it in any medium by electronic means and whether or not transiently or incidentally to some
other use of this publication) without the written permission of the copyright owner, except in accordance with the
provisions of the Copyright, Designs and Patents Act 1988 or under the terms of a licence issued by the Copyright
Licensing Agency, Barnards Inn, 86 Fetter Lane, London EC4A 1EN (http://www.cla.co.uk). Applications for the
copyright owner's written permission should be addressed to the publisher.

Printed in the UK by Bell & Bain Ltd, Glasgow

For Power Maths resources go to
www.activelearnprimary.co.uk

Note from the publisher
Pearson has robust editorial processes, including answer and fact checks, to ensure the accuracy of the content in this
publication, and every effort is made to ensure this publication is free of errors. We are, however, only human, and
occasionally errors do occur. Pearson is not liable for any misunderstandings that arise as a result of errors in this
publication, but it is our priority to ensure that the content is accurate. If you spot an error, please do contact us at
resourcescorrections@pearson.com so we can make sure it is corrected.